TO TALK OF MANY THINGS: SELECTED POEMS

 A catalogue record for this book is available from the National Library of Australia

© Richard Greene

Published 2021

ISBN: 978-0-6453437-5-5 (epub)
ISBN: 978-0-6453437-6-2 (paperback)
ISBN: 978-0-6453437-7-9 (PDF)

Published with the aid of Jumble Books and Publishers
(jumblebooksandpublishers.com)

To Talk of Many Things

Selected Poems

by

Richard Greene

Image Credit:
'A scene from "The Walrus and the Carpenter", by Lewis Carroll, drawn by Sir John Tenniel in 1871.'
Also known as 'Briny Beach'.
This image is in the public domain.

Contents

Memories 1
To the Basement and Back 2
West Side Memories 3
Pullman Memories 4
Watermelon Days 7
Under the Apple Boughs 8
World's Fair 10
Milkmen 11
Where Have the Hurdy-gurdy Men Gone? 12
First Tug 13
A World That Was 14
September 1, 1939 15
Growing Up 16
Early Explorer 17
Seventeen 19
Becoming T. S. Eliot 20
Driving to the Sun 21
Birthday 22
My Daughter 23
To My Son 24
Metamorphosis 25
Mother's Day 26
Pie 27
Soccer Season 28
Skipping 29
The Crew 30
Once More into the Breach 31
Men of Stature 32
My Age of Aquarius 33
My Third-grade Playmates 35
The End of the Race 36
On the Downhill Side 37
I See Myself Becoming Old 38

Their Jungle Gym Is Overgrown with Vines 40
Ossuary 41
Play Jolly Music at My Funeral 42
Our Love 43
Last Words 45
A Woman's Laughter 46
Built of Words 47
Married Life 48
Silver Is the Color of My True Love's Hair 49
I Like a Woman with Wrinkles 50
Marblehead 51
The Housatonic Near Kent 53
The Lake at Evening 54
One of Those Rare Moments 55
There's Something About a Lake 56
Seeing Water 57
Cotapaxi 60
The View from Berkeley 61
Orinocos of the Imagination 62
Surrounded by the Universe 63
Rain 64
In the Park 65
The River 66
Geometry 67
By the Plain of Jezreel 68
Riverworld 69
To the Source 70
At the Beach 71
Ode to an Island 73
Rievaulx Abbey 74
Pemaquid Point 75
The Lake 76
Overture 78
County Fair 79
Clouds 80

The Kite	81
Rowing at Evening	82
Floating World	83
Lamb-white Days	84
Rainy Evening Near the Hudson	85
The Bridge	86
Forsaken City	87
Winter Brilliance	88
Moon Madness	89
Birds of a Feather	90
A Chicken's Lot	91
Evermore	92
Sound Effects	93
Cousin Gull	94
Bird Love	95
Grackles	97
Crows in the Rain	99
Early Birds	100
Geese on the Loose	101
Man and Dog	102
Guinevere	103
Dogs/Cats	104
Room with Cats	105
Cat and Geese	106
Children's Story	107
Rhapsody in Butterflies	109
Burros	110
Carriage Horses	111
Apple Factory	112
The Climbing Tree	113
Trees	114
What the March Wind Saw	115
On the Verge	116
The First Flower of Spring	117
Signs of April	118

Mildred Munsees Spring	119
Spring Snow	120
Rite of Spring	121
Spring Surge	122
Let the Season Begin	123
Processional	124
Here Comes the Parade	125
Pyrotechnics	126
April Is the Cruelest Month	127
Pioneer	128
Crayon Work	129
Awakenings	130
It's in the Air	131
Frabjous Day	132
Firefly Time	133
Independence Day	134
Summer Is Here Now	135
Summer Morning	136
Midsummer Day	137
Summer Shadows	138
Summer Symphony	139
Summer's End	140
Yesterday Was the Last Day of Summer	141
Autumn Road	142
A Time of Falling Leaves	143
October Morning	144
It Was One of Those Fine October Days	145
The Beach in Autumn	146
Green and Dying	147
Indian Summer	148
The Days Grow Shorter	149
North Wind	150
Strike up the Band	151
Football Weather	152
Autumn Riff	153

Autumn Sonata	154
Those Days	155
November Afternoon	156
Above the Valley	157
First Snow	158
Homage to Omar Khayyam	159
First Snow, December	160
December Snow	161
Season's Greetings	162
Snowfall	163
Deep Snow	164
Chicago Winter	165
Inching up on the Equinox	166
First Notes	167
Last Snow	168
Still Delighting in Snow	169
Winter's End	170
Everyday Things	171
Old Furnace	172
Smiles	173
Pudding	174
Polished Stones	175
Poetry in the Suburbs	176
The Quiet Life	177
The Reading	178
Li Po	179
Life and Death	180
Confession	181
Painting with Words	182
Functional Family	183
Not Much of an American	184
Progress	185
Developing Eden	186
After the Fall	187
A Manatee Comes to Manhattan	188

Out of an Economy Endlessly Growing	189
Angst	193
Rationalizing for God	194
Book and Other Worms	195
A Man for Some Seasons	196
Aftermath	200
Remembering Vientiane	201
The Veterans	202
All the Brave Men	203
Where Have All the Young Men Gone?	204
The Grenade	205
The Weapons Economy	206
A Boy's War	207
The Charms of War	208
In Memory of	209
I Was a Soldier Once	210
The Things They Carry	211
Memorial	212
Memorial Day	213
December 7, 1941	216
September 1, 1939	217
The Unnamed Dead	218
Your Grandfather's War	219
To Those without Whom We Couldn't Win	221
Beauty and Truth	222
Of Frogs and Toads	223
The Competitive Society	224
Yom HaShoah	225
Earthquake, Port-au-Prince, 2010	226
Nothing New	227
Mankind and Moonshine	229
The Afterlife of Gods	230
Faking It	231
The Hospital Poem	233
Existentially Speaking	235

Hello, Is Polly There Please? 236
Timepieces 237
The Sun and the Moon 238
Tall Ships 239
Islands of the Mind 240
Wild Things 241
Of Roosters and Motorcars 242
The Bag 243
The Bear 244
The Inner Child 245
Words 246
Intimate Strangers 247
Wind 248
I Hear Its Whistle 249
Thinking of Teachers 250
Where Are You Now, Shirley Temple? 251
The Theater Is Closed 252
Old Barn 253
The Voices of Stones 254
Sunday on the Bike Path 255
TRANSLATIONS 257
Ave Atque Vale—Catullus 257
VIII—Catullus 258
An Old and Distinguished Gentleman—Antonio Machado 259
November 1913—Antonio Machado 260
Autumn Day—Rainer Marie Rilke 261
Black Cat—Rainer Marie Rilke 262

To Mrs. McCracken, my 8th grade English teacher, the late Henry Rago, one time editor of *Poetry* magazine who, as one of my professors at the University of Chicago, encouraged me in my poetry writing, and to my wife, Celeste, who has supported and encouraged me in many ways, not least with regard to my poetry, copyediting my poems and making helpful suggestions.

Memories

I don't need more memories
yet they keep coming.
Nearly seventy years accumulation stored away
in the attics, closets, cupboards of my mind,
but more arrive each day,
and the bedchambers too are full
of animated guests.
Granted, some don't stay,
and some stay only awhile
taking their leave considerately.
Others, however, remain,
stalking the halls year after year,
some unremarkable,
some congenial,
some unwelcome lodgers who resist eviction.
And so, though the house is full
it keeps on filling
for it seems there's no end
to the memories it can hold.
    (May 13, 2000)

To the Basement and Back

Looking for something in the basement this
    morning
I noticed once state-of-the-art equipment I'll
    never use again,
which reminded me
of other phantoms that haunt my nether world,
paint that no longer adorns our walls,
gadgets whose use I no longer know,
the too-warm sheepskin coat I never wear,
still-good suitcases
supplanted by newer ones that won my favor,
books I'll almost certainly never read again, nor
    lend,
a book I was going to return but never did
which reminded me in turn
of friends I meant to call,
but weeks turned into months
and months into years,
and I came back upstairs
bearing the baggage of those years.
    (April 13, 2002)

West Side Memories

We lived across from the planetarium,
mere yards from the sky,
while just down the street
was the el,
and still vivid
under the long-gone girders,
a barbershop
with its candy stripe pole
and carousel pony
astride which young clients sat,
at the center of the universe.
    (July 1998)

Pullman Memories

Riding a train
takes me back
to those boyhood summers
when I traveled alone
from New York to Chicago
starting from Grand Central Station
with a gentle jolt,
gathering momentum
past the vacant eyed apartments
of upper Manhattan,
wondering about the people
who lived inside,
then over to the river
where we hit full stride,
our wheels clicking
at a Dixieland pace,
the Hudson Valley scrolling by,
lake-wide river, stubs of old mountain,
the play of light in a cloud-crowded sky,
until we turned off at Albany
into mile on mile of farms and woods,
imagining myself into the houses
along the right of way,
those who might live within
seeming not quite real,
as we no doubt to them,
two worlds
sliding by one another
each in its own continuum
of time and space.

Then in the dining car,
self-conscious but proud,
the center of attention
in that adult place,
and not long after
in my berth,
snug as a tent,
shaken down to sleep
by the jiggling of the train,
waking during the night
when we stopped
at some anonymous station,
pulling the window shade up a crack
to see if I could make out a sign
of where we were,
watching the moving figures
swathed in steam,
silhouetted against the platform lights.

Then it was morning
and the flat fields of Indiana
were wheeling by,
telephone poles
riffling by
at a dizzy pace.
Like a horse
galloping back to its stable,
we seemed to accelerate
as we drew near our destination.
I felt I had to hurry getting dressed
lest I would still be in my pajamas
when we reached Dearborn Station

where the train might be shunted off
before I emerged,
my father on the platform muttering,
"Where is that boy?"
But we slowed down
as we swam into the denser urban landscape
and instead of being caught unprepared
I waited impatiently
for that endless city
to end.
    (February 1999)

Watermelon Days

Here I am, a graybeard, eating watermelon
and remembering those summers
when I could count my age in single digits,
summers at the lake where my grandfather had a
 house
and all the cousins would assemble for dinner
around my grandmother's large table.
Though there's plenty of melon in the fridge
I find myself cutting close to the rind,
as I did in those days,
and there I am,
still that boy at seventy-three,
at the table with the tiffany lamp overhead
or descending the hill to the lake,
its remembered water, smooth and green,
lapping softly on the shore,
and the sound of mourning doves in
 counterpoint.
    (August 23, 2004)

Under the Apple Boughs

There was a wall along the road
where we played soldier
behind the loosely stacked stones.
Next to it a row of mountain birch
tops tinted in memory with evening sun.
Then the house
in dappled coat of whitewashed brick,
and the orchard with gnarled trees
where we pressed apples on chill fall days
and savored the cold, sweet cider.

Outside my bedroom window
a camellia tree glistened,
and, beyond, a broad lawn
sloped down to the pond
where frogs held nightly congress
and I learned of mallards
and snapping turtles
and green-winged teals.
There we skated in winter
until darkness hid the agate surface,
and swam impatiently in spring,
the ice barely melted,
as if our innocence protected us from cold.

Between pond and house
stood a lone apple tree
where, as I watched at first light,
pheasants gathered

in their courtly plumage
to feast on windfalls.

Then bombs fell on Pearl Harbor
and soldier games gave way to war.
	(September 1998)

World's Fair
"You may not be interested in war, but war is interested in you."—Leon Trotsky

I went to my first world's fair
when I was eight.
As is the way with such events
it was more about us
than the world,
and refracted the future
through optimist eyes.
You wouldn't have known
from anything on display
that a cancer festered
in Europe's bosom
or that the most brutal of wars
was mere months away.
Nor was there any inkling
of the baleful new words
soon to be unleashed
on our vocabulary,
blitzkrieg, storm trooper, quisling,
kamikaze, Hiroshima,
Holocaust,
while the Futurama
with its ebullient guides
depicted a morrow
of shining towers
where poverty was ostracized.
Oh, the world looked good
in our neighborhood
in the spring of '39.
    (March 10, 2000)

Milkmen

This morning I dreamt of the milkmen
who used to deploy through the half-lit city,
when I was a child,
with their cargo of clean, white liquid
and rows of glistening bottles,
depositing their burden
on doorsteps and porches
with a soft clinking
that made sleep
all the more voluptuous.

This morning I dreamt of milkmen,
but, when I awoke,
they were only a dream.
  (September 10, 1999)

Where Have the Hurdy-gurdy Men Gone?

Reader, do you even know what they were,
the knife sharpeners, the milkmen, the icemen,
who peopled the world of my youth?
Have they all quite faded away,
or is there an alternative universe
where crowds of them circle in the streets
performing the slow waltz of time?
    (July 8, 2005)

First Tug

"I've got a fish" I shouted.
I was five,
gone fishing with my father
in his boat with oars I tried
but couldn't manage.
It seemed such a long time I sat there
dangling a worm in the water,
the boat gently rocking
in the drowsy summer sunshine,
when suddenly there was a tug on my line,
that first tug
of a lifetime.
    (May 19, 2000)

A World That Was

As I turn on the radio
this Saturday afternoon
opera swells out
from where I left the dial
and I'm transmitted back
more than half the century
to those peaceful prewar days
when I had no intimation
of what the future held,
and our radio
with its gothic wooden case
was tuned to the Met
in our living room.

I associated opera in those days
with dull times
when I was housebound
and would restlessly quarter
that thicket of sound
chafing for something to do.
For years after
I never cared much for opera,
but it sings to me now
of a world that was,
in a child's hopeful eyes.
      (October 17, 1999)

September 1, 1939

Where was I?
At home in our tranquil suburb?
In school, or was it too soon?
Playing with friends?
Reading in my room?
Still at the lake perhaps
or on a train
coming home.
I don't know what time of day it was,
don't think I even heard the news.
My parents surely knew
but they must have said
best not tell the children.
Nor did I know of Kristallnacht
Munich
the Sudetenland
Anschluss.

It was probably summery still,
the leaves unchanged,
a calm September day.
    (March 10, 2007)

Growing Up

While I was growing up in a comfortable suburb
a million and a half children
Jews like myself
died in camps,
not like the ones where I passed my summers.
While I dallied down the tree-lined street to
   school
past big houses and spacious yards
those other children
were turned out of their schools and homes.
While I studied Hebrew and piano lackadaisically
those other children learned firsthand
the meaning of the Kaddish and the dirge.
While I pushed away the food
my grandmother urged on me
those other children grew thin
till they seemed not much more than skeletons.
And while I lay in my familiar bed
in my lovingly furnished room
fretting, perhaps, about a catch I'd flubbed,
but nonetheless falling asleep easily,
those other children slept fitfully
disturbed by barrack sounds
and nightmares of men in jackboots
and the smoke from chimneys.
     (June 29, 2003)

Early Explorer

Living in L.A.
when it was much smaller than today
I ranged far
on my balloon-tire Schwinn
from our suburban fastness
eastward down the daylong boulevard
rolling the city's length,
like LaSalle
exploring the great mid-continental waterway,
past movie houses
and department stores
full of siren temptations,
past buildings monotonous as waves
toward the city's towered center
which I saw each time longingly from afar
but reached only once
having to turn back time and again
to be home before dark,

westward toward the ocean,
that shore I never reached,
picturing its blue expanse
with dogged anticipation
as I toiled my way
past mile on mile
of urban Gobi,

or over the high hills to the north
through untamed canyons
with their boulder strewn streams

and groves of scrub oak
to the range's far shoulders
overlooking a broad valley
that reached into the blue-gray distance
(imagining myself a pioneer surmounting
the last westward fold of the Sierra)
then down to the citrus groves
where I lingered
among multitudes of orange globes
in the welcoming shade.
    (January 16, 2000)

Seventeen

That summer I worked at a camp
not far from the city
on the other side of the river.
One of the counselors, Didi—
Shirly Lutz, from Akron Ohio—
was a lithe, compact girl
with a sweet smell of sunlight about her,
and as she sat in the high lifeguard chair,
her smooth legs crossed,
the guys would crowd around
like stage door Johnnies
vying for attention.

Didi and I had the same night off
and we'd go into the city
down to the Village
and all-night smoky jazz,
heading back to camp
not long before dawn
taking the nearly empty subway
to the bridge.
The buses didn't run at that hour
so we'd walk the mile across,
solitary voices
high above the water,
the sun rising at our backs,
our shadows stretching out
long as the life before us.
(July 15, 1999)

Becoming T. S. Eliot

When I was young and impressionable
I wanted to be T. S. Eliot.
No matter that I didn't understand much of his
  poetry.
I felt a man of letters was the most admirable
  thing to be.
As for the physical heroes of yore,
I knew that wasn't me,
and, having been "poet laureate" of my eighth
  grade class,
I aspired to emulate
that paragon of modernity.
The first step I took
was to get horn-rimmed glasses
though it was arguable whether I needed glasses
  yet.
An aunt of mine said to me
with amazing perspicacity
(though she never even went to college)
"You may think they make you look intellectual,
but you'll have to wear them the rest of your life."
I kept them anyway
and wear glasses still
but, as far as I can tell,
they've done nothing for my poetry.
    (May 22, 2003)

Driving to the Sun

From Paris
to the Costa del Sol
we drove
in my dilapidated convertible
in the springtime of our lives
down a long, straight Roman road
tunneling through pines
on into Spain
drifting through Madrid, Granada, Sevilla
then to Málaga
the top down
Colette and Serge
perched on the seat backs
waving to the earthbound
as we sailed through small towns
on our way to the sky.
    (July 15, 1999)

Birthday

Dawn rose this morning on a clear sky
bearing only a few cupcakes of cloud
but gilded by a billion candle light.
Today I'm seventy-five.
   (March 23, 2006)

My Daughter

My daughter,
thirteen
but looking twelve,
still a child
while other girls
are becoming women,
walks to the school door
with a faintly jerky step
toes pointing slightly outward.

She looks vulnerable,
or is it that I know
she's teased
and feel
a fierce desire
to protect her.
    (September 1984)

To My Son

I was there
when you were squeezed
from your mother's womb,
coming into this world
not like a deity,
clean, calm and complete,
but as a man does,
red, wrinkled and vulnerable,
looking bewildered and indignant,
like a turtle deprived of its shell.
    (March 1999)

Metamorphosis

She was thirteen,
more erect in her bearing
sparer in her movements
graver in speech
careful of her dignity,
but occasionally
when younger girls
surrounded her
she would revert
to childish ways
joining coltishly
in their play.
(June 11, 1999)

Mother's Day

Two young mothers at the pool
acquaint their progeny with aquatics
that they should be confident in the water,
maybe even champions one day.
The mothers converse,
babies attached to their hips
like accessories,
smiling much at each other
and their children even more.
After a while
they place their offspring
on the pool's edge
carefully, as one might put a glass bowl
back on a gift shop shelf,
continuing to grasp them firmly
as they talk.
The babies
one a boy, one a girl,
but too young to appreciate the difference,
sit in the tile gutter
gurgling like the water,
absorbed in their half-formed worlds.
    (September 22, 2000)

Pie

Apple, blueberry, cherry, peach,
coconut custard, banana cream,
boyhood's soft-focus dreams.

I used to stop at the bakery
on the way home from school
to buy an individual pie
one just the size for a boy
but an aunt with whom I stayed for a while
forbade me them,
deeming pies bad for one's health.
Seeing me once munching one
as I ambled home from school
she gave me a scolding so fierce
I flinch from it to this day
when pie is forbidden me again
under the strictures of age.

Shades of Simple Simon,
Tom Sawyer, Huckleberry Finn,
and maybe Adam too,
for what do you suppose was his favorite dish
after that first taste of sin?
Which leads me to a metaphysical question,
was pie designed for boys
or boys for pie?
    (May 27, 2006)

Soccer Season

September 1,
gray and unseasonably cool,
as if autumn were already here,
I drive by the high school playing field
where the portable soccer goals are out.
Images of picking up my son after practice.
His birthday's today.
He's thirty-three
and I picture him now,
six inches taller than me,
with broad shoulders, long nose,
and wide mouth,
bent in an ironic smile,
and inside the image of the man
a much smaller one
with the gently angled features of a child.
    (September 1, 2006)

Skipping

I saw a child skipping
and thought to myself
how long it's been since I've skipped.
Since I was a child, I suppose,
before I was weighed down with gravity
and gravitas.
 (February 25, 2010)

The Crew

A crew is out for early practice
caressing the morning air
with rapt strokes
cleaving the smooth water
with rhythmic thrusts
feeling no doubt
it's good to be young
and drowsily awake
stretched out on a long-limbed river
this fine spring morning.
    (June 8, 1999)

Once More into the Breach

Even the most venerable of men,
statesmen, generals, philosophers
even clergymen
even men of letters,
buttocks waving naked in the air,
grunting, heaving, sweating, groaning, quivering
without a thought for dignity,
policy, strategy,
philosophy, theology or art,
with thought for nothing, in fact,
all leveled in feeling,
literary light and hack
field marshal and corporal
highbrow and lowbrow
writer and reader
I and thou,
all plunging in the dark.
    (May 28, 2000)

Men of Stature

All these men of stature,
the statesman, the judge, the general, the dictator
the titan, the tycoon, the magnate, the mogul
the bishop, the pope, the ayatollah
the philosopher, the laureate,
all were once infants
lying on their small backs
kicking aimlessly
grabbing handfuls of air
feeding from a teat,
were once small boys
mixing up their words
unable to cross the street alone,
then, a bit older,
with clear skin, piping voices
and still childish repartee,
and adolescents
contrary, sullen, unsure of themselves
driven by the fever in their loins.

You wouldn't have imagined
that these boys would one day be
men of stature.
Nor is it easy to imagine now
that they once were young and vulnerable.
    (October 30, 2002)

My Age of Aquarius

I happened to look at a picture
that's been hanging in our house for years
but seldom engages my awareness.
The picture's a drawing by my friend Lenny
of his wife Esther
pregnant and sitting on a bed, sewing.
It's from some forty years ago.

We were in Ecuador,
I working for our government
and Lennie escaping
from the materialism of American life,
or maybe the draft.
In photos from that time
I'm wearing long sideburns
and granny glasses.

So Lennie and I were pals.
He introduced me to pot
(I wasn't very precocious that way)
and I remember a moonlit night
we grooved on a chain link fence.

Esther was pregnant with Yamara,
a Quechua Indian name.
They later had a boy named Sparrow
who'd be in his thirties now.
I've wondered from time to time
how he fared with that name.

I heard that Lennie and Esther divorced,
but that was after I last saw them,
over a generation
and four Republican presidents ago.
    (January 13, 2009)

My Third-grade Playmates

My third-grade playmates are 68.
Smooth skin has withered.
Nimble bodies have grown tentative.
Voices once fluting now grate.
Dreams have curdled.
Ambition is in disrepair.
They are full of memories
and in memory they are preserved.
The children of my memory
are old.
    (January 2, 2000)

The End of the Race

For much of our lives we wish we could hurry
 time,
become one of the older kids,
then an adult,
graduate,
end the week's work sooner,
gallop to an anticipated holiday or anniversary,
shorten the wait for a child to be born,
and we're pleased when time seems to run flat
 out.

Then one day we notice
the end of the course is in sight
and we'd like to slow down.
But time keeps cantering
at its habitual pace
immune to rein and spur alike
and what seemed so slow before
now seems all too fast.
  (October 1, 2000)

On the Downhill Side

April is almost over
having, it seems, only just begun.
Once past the apex
we speed ever faster.
Ascending was slower
The landscape labored by.
Each time you rounded a curve
there was another just ahead
and you never saw the summit
much less the decline on the other side.
Then one day you notice you're on the
   downgrade.
The landscape unreels
at an accelerating pace.
You glimpse lowlands in the distance
from time to time
but the road
absorbed in its curves
never reveals its destination.
Down you go
wind pressed to your face,
applying the brakes
which no longer work the way they used to
and the last thing on your mind
is to shout whoopee.
   (April 30, 2001)

I See Myself Becoming Old

My closet is full of suits I don't wear anymore.
Nothing I need to wear them for.
There are days when I stay in my pajamas till
    noon.
I picture my heirs looking at my wardrobe one
    day
asking "Can you think of anyone who can use
    these
or should we give them to Goodwill?"
Or, "Would you like this tie as a remembrance of
    Dad?"
As I read the obits of the recently deceased,
which I took to doing a few years ago,
I compare their ages to mine.

Then there's the arthritis in my hands and feet.
My left foot aches when I walk
and I suffered a rupture in a time-worn tendon
    not long ago.
I have more trouble lifting things and getting
    around.
Don't jump over puddles anymore
for fear of the damage I might do coming down.
(No more kicking up heels for me.)

What will it be next,
the incipient cataracts?
My hearing isn't what it used to be.
I don't think I need a hearing aid yet,
though my daughter disagrees.

Or will it be something unforeseen
like that ill-fated tendon?

I see myself becoming old,
yet it's as if I were watching it happen to
 somebody else.
  (October 23, 2003)

Their Jungle Gym Is Overgrown with Vines

In the house
there's a bedroom, I imagine,
or more than one perhaps,
preserved as a museum,
on the walls posters of decades past,
surfaces otherwise uncluttered
beds always neatly made,
and those who remain behind,
their hair gradually turning gray.
    (December 1, 2009)

Ossuary

Rubbing my arthritic hands I notice
the skeleton inside.
It's as though the flesh were retracting
revealing bone,
but more likely
I've merely become conscious,
as befits my age,
of being a soft receptacle
that will soon biodegrade.
      (December 5, 2009)

Play Jolly Music at My Funeral

I've taken in recent years to thinking about my
 funeral
and have decided to make one paramount
 request;
play jolly music at that ritual.
What good does it do to heap on dirges
or other mournful melodies?
I won't be there to be gratified by the grieving
and if I could tune in
I'd be happier to see those present have some
 relief.
Jelly Roll would be nice.
Joplin would be fine.
Something by Fats Waller would certainly do.
Those early jazzmen knew what they were up to
when they set about making funeral marches
 swing.
So swing me away, please, with a rousing tune.
 (May 19, 2004)

Our Love

Our love burns gently,
more candle than torch,
but enduring,
like the miraculous lamp
in the temple.

Our love is no mountain
rearing above the Earth
for all to see
but rather a more modest monument,
like those mounds
evidencing the long presence
of human life,
an accumulation of small moments;
hearing you at the door
in the evening
when you return from work,
reaching out to touch you
when I lie down in bed at night,
squeezing your thigh
in the enthusiasm
of being together
as we start off on a trip.

Our love isn't electric.
It doesn't jolt,
though it powers
with the slow steadiness of water
turning a mill wheel.

Undramatic, some would scoff,
but they confuse
the pleasures of watching drama
with the ordeal of living it.
      (January 1999)

Last Words

I'm ready to cross the river now
on this rickety raft of bones
in this bag of sagging skin.
Let me swim.
All my life I've swum
beginning in the womb.
Now's no time
to start riding in boats.
      (September 14, 1999)

A Woman's Laughter

defies gravity
brightens a cloudy day
makes the dog wag its tail
    the child grow,
    man submit.
(March 1999)

Built of Words

Let's kiss and make up, we say,
putting our lips together
to mend a breach,
as if they were a bridge
between the islands we can be.
An embrace can serve as well
but words
are the most enduring of all,
bridge or wall.
     (August 24, 1999)

Married Life

You have a husband.
I have a wife.
We know what conjugal life is like,
the united front
the tug of war
the complementary anatomy.
    (April 2, 2006)

Silver Is the Color of My True Love's Hair

as if some cunning craftsman
had spun metal
into silken thread.
It was chestnut brown when we met.
Her skin, all smooth then,
has begun to show fine webs
and is slack under her once firm chin.
But, when I look on her, I think
this is the girl I wed
and feel the need to kiss her cheek
or, if she's bent over some task,
the nape of her neck
or, if she's sitting with the hem of her dress
resting on her thighs,
to reach out and touch her knee.
   (June 13, 2009)

I Like a Woman with Wrinkles

being of wrinkly age myself.
It's as if we were fellow immigrants
in the country of the young,
the fresh faced
and so often self-absorbed,
with their new enthusiasms
which they fancy
set the standards for all time.
No, give me a woman who knows
how fashions come and go
who's earned her wrinkles
with toil and grief
with whom I can empathize,
and compare notes.
    (March 20, 2010)

Marblehead

Sun spangled
sail flecked
homespun bay,
cloud bannered
beach blazoned,
yes wine dark too,

a fanfare of trumpets
and cellos,
the somber brilliance
of a northern sea.
(August 1974)

Titicaca

the lake
astonishingly blue
in the mouth of *nevados*
that poke like teeth
through the dry land

a creature in whose throat
one sees the cosmos
      (July 1991)

The Housatonic Near Kent

Slowly
the river unwinds
through flat fields,
scarcely stirring the reeds,
its voice not even a murmur.

Fish hang
in the hushed flow
weightless as shadows.
    (July 1996)

The Lake at Evening

The sky is still,
the water too,
hushed,
expectant,
as the worldlight dims
and trees silhouette
a watery stage
where fish dimple
the plainsong surface
and birds pirouette
through the gilded air.
      (September 1996)

One of Those Rare Moments

It was one of those rare moments
when the Earth holds its breath,
the air is utterly still
and lakes are transformed into mirrors
reflecting sky and trees
with serene precision.
 (December 1998)

There's Something About a Lake

the mysteries
beneath its surface;
its alien inhabitants
in their alien world;
its changing moods and attire,
vivacious blue,
tranquil green,
somber gray;
garments plain
or ornamented
with wind whipped lace
or sequins of sunlight;
calm as a monk in meditation,
contorted with stormy anger,
or performing its glad dance
under a sunny sky.

There's something about a lake
that plays on our hearts and minds.
      (January 1999)

Seeing Water

Even now, in my sixty-eighth year,
I still experience a thrill
when rounding a curve
or topping a hill
I come upon a body of water,
whether festive blue
or sullen gray,
open to view
or half hidden by trees.
Even a small lake
I pass almost every day
still surprises me
with a pulse of pleasure.
It summons up, I suppose,
the lake where I spent
my childhood summers,
its mile-wide waters
abloom with sails,
where I fished
as day segued into night
and gold streaked
the sky's book of hours,

the remote Canadian lakes
where I basked in a solitude
broken only by the lonely cry of loons,
moose grazing in the shallows
or the occasional band of Cree
in their quiet canoes,
gathering wild rice,

and overhead at night
the sky-spanning, pulsating
polychrome curtain
of the aurora,

or the Hudson
where I whiled away my time
watching ships slide languorously by,
the slow kaleidoscope
of clouds and sky
over the Jersey bank,
or seagulls
gliding against the towering Palisades
so steady on their wings
the world seemed to move
while they stood still,
and in the background always
the tremendous harp of the bridge
gracing the river's canyon
as it might the very gates of heaven.

Then there's the Pacific
which, more precocious than Balboa,
I first saw at age six,
having come from the east
with my grandmother
who, indulging me,
drove straight to the water,
not even stopping
at our new home.
It was overcast that day
and I was disappointed

that the great ocean
wasn't the least bit blue.
Still, it was the Pacific,
spreading all the way
from California to Cathay
with a leap
only the imagination could equal.
    (January 1999)

Cotapaxi

Just below a great snowy cone in the Andes
on a broad, flat shelf of mountain
wild horses race
keeping pace
with wind-driven clouds overhead,
breath steaming
long manes swirling,
exhilarated,
as if created
just moments before
out of the primordial chaos.
    (February 1999)

The View from Berkeley

Fog awakens
to a rising sun
on a sheet of shale green bay,
stretches,
uncovering the comely shoulders
of Mount Tamalpais,
slides down
the taut tendons of the bridge,
but leaves the city's towers
still half veiled,
as it slowly, slowly rises
from its bed.
    (April 1999)

Orinocos of the Imagination

I've never been to the Orinoco
and have seen few photos of it,
but I feel I know its sinuous lengths,
winding between thick jungle walls,
flashing silver in the sun,
delicate waterfalls
threading from cloud-shrouded cliffs,
dense foliage
adorned with birds of kindergarten colors
and jaguars that merge into shadow,
the insistent music
of bird cry and monkey chatter,
dugouts and caimans
scoring its sleek waters,
those who people its valley
gliding nearly naked
through twilight forests,
dappled by the distant sun.
I know these lush landscapes
from my dreams.
    (May 23, 1999)

Surrounded by the Universe

In these early morning hours
in this room
it begins
stretching outward
from the circle of lamplight on my desk
to the leaf-dappled streetlight across the way
to the moon's chalky mirror
to the distant incandescence of the stars,
from the scratch of my pen
to the scrapings of insects in surrounding fields
to the faint but ceaseless aura of traffic sounds
through the intermittent silences of space
to the obliterating but unheard stellar roar,
and so to the dead-quiet edges of this universe
where starlight thins to blackness,
from the small circle of lamplight
on my desk.
    (June 4, 1999)

Rain

tumbling, teeming, driving
rustling, rumbling, gurgling
tapping, pounding, thrumming, drumming
splattering, splashing, spraying
puddling, pooling, rushing.
Rain,
this hurricane.
(September 16, 1999)

In the Park

Idlers and lovers,
readers and sleepers,
clerks in blouses and skirts
or crisp shirts and creased trousers,
T-shirted workmen with long hair and tattoos,
ebullient sales girls,
bored matrons,
boys with ominous eyes,
sharp-eyed young men in expensive suits,
young mothers wheeling carriages
or with toddlers in tow,
dog walkers harnessed to their canines,
children engrossed in their play,
families in affectionate embrace,
equestrians and their mounts
in intimate symbiosis,
bikers, skaters, skate boarders, joggers,
all in appropriate apparel,
diverse ballplayers,
speakers of many tongues,
kite flyers and Frisbee flingers,
boaters, sunbathers, vendors,
pigeons and picnickers,
peace officers and perps,
house cats, squirrels, chipmunks,
ducks, geese, hawks, sparrows,
bees, ants, flies,
all crowd into the park.
    (November 20, 1999)

The River

We don't often think
beside a small stream,
a brook we can straddle,
of the great river
in might become,
the ocean
into which it might empty,
flowing away clear
over its pebbled bed,
white flecked
down a perseverant slope,
over falls
through forests
gathering bulk and muscle
through farmlands
past towns
becoming broader
and darker,
past cities
that bridge and bind
yet cannot fully tame it,
then free
into the welcoming arms
of bay or estuary
and at last to the ocean,
like a son come back
from long wanderings.
    (December 28, 1999)

Geometry

Another cloud shrouded winter morning.
Raindrops bead the windowpanes
refracting a dusky landscape
where streetlights still shine
enclosed in luminous spheres of rain
while at my desk
a cone of lamplight
pierces the enveloping darkness.
    (January 10, 2000)

By the Plain of Jezreel

Once by the plain of Jezreel
across from the well of Gideon
where trumpets filled the night
across from Mount Gilboa
where Saul and his three sons died
I climbed a hill
and on the other side
saw hills ranging far and wide
over the Jordan and into the land beyond,
and heard voices in the wind.
    (March 4, 2000)

Riverworld

Where the small midwestern river
issued from its lake
running smooth and brown
under a translucent vault of willows
I went exploring
when I was ten or so
imagining myself a voyageur
descending the mighty Mississippi.

There I encountered exotic fauna,
catfish with their mandarin whiskers,
looking learned and wise,
mud-puppies emerging from the water
like the first sea creatures
venturing onto land.

There sandy banks
sank into sepia waters
and a sunlit world
was steeped in mystery.
    (June 12, 2000)

To the Source

I've lived near the river's end,
where its wide waters slide
into bay and ocean,
and watched ships ride the deep water.
Often I've dreamed
of tracing it to its source
past the farthest reach of ocean vessels,
past stretches where the silken flow
is trimmed with frothy white
and you can see the mountains' bones
beneath the water,
climbing, ever climbing
through field and forest
at last to the place,
in a watery meadow perhaps
or hidden under trees,
where the great river is born,
issuing from the earth
in a stream so small
you could cup it in your hands.
    (July 31, 2000)

At the Beach

Summers at the beach
we turned pink on the yellow sand
wore grit like a second skin
fast high-stepped to the water
on sand sometimes so hot
we tried to run without touching ground,
splashed into the cooling water
tasting its brine
our nostrils full of that scent
that told us where we were
when we first drew near the shore,
swam out to waves
that carried us headlong on their crests
whirling us down as they crumbled
supplying us with breathless tales
when we were back on land.
Then we walked on the wet sand
where water followed in our footprints
while we gathered shells and sand dollars
and flat, smooth stones
rounded by the tireless work of water,
and watched white-vested gulls,
those dapper beachcombers,
waddle down the strand
or, balancing on a breeze,
glide down the shore
like notes of an arpeggio.

Then late in the day
when we were tired and the tide came in,
mesmerized by the ocean's pulse

we watched it rise on the beach,
dissolving sand castles,
so painstakingly wrought,
then, nonchalantly, slide back down,
and at night
the timeless sound of breaking waves
lulled us to sleep.
    (August 5, 2000)

Ode to an Island

My sister lives on a Caribbean isle,
little more than a dust mote on a map,
no realm of magic,
nor Ariel, nor Caliban
(though a touch of each),
no stage for grand drama,
merely the familiar theater of domesticity,

but birds flower there
and flowers take flight,
fish flash rainbows over the coral,
palm fronds sway to the wind
as if spellbound in dance,
and in the night
as you drift into sleep
you hear the waves upon the reef
intoning the ancient anthem of the sea.
    (December 27, 2001)

Rievaulx Abbey

Once filled with glowing glass,
its tall arches
are full now with the green of fields and trees.
Sunlight plays in the empty nave,
the sky for a roof,
a shifting panorama,
Wedgwood blue with cameo clouds,
fretted by passing birds,
or dark but pierced with stars.
Wind, rain and snow freely flow
where worshippers once kneeled.
The altar is a knoll,
wild flowers the congregation.
    (May 28, 2005)

Pemaquid Point

You feel the force of the ocean here,
the wind driven waves
pounding the water white,
fraying the land's rocky edges,
even holding the season back,
the leaves still small and pale here,
now in this middle of May.

You feel the water's weight and breadth,
filling the deep Atlantic basin,
stretching to far-away continents
under many-hued skies.
    (May 14, 2006)

The Lake

There was a lake in Michigan
where I spent my childhood summers,
a glacial lake
with hilly banks
scooped out of flat farmland.
A mile wide and three long,
it was big enough
for the far shore to seem a foreign place,
adding to the mystery of the water
with its large carp that hovered in the shallows
    like blimps
and its murky depths,
tall seaweed reaching up at you
as you swam into the deep water
where there were primitive slashing carnivores
alligator gar
rumored to have once attacked a man.

But there were also the sunfish and bluegills,
their rainbow hues visible in the shallows,
bass, streamlined and speckled,
minnows that would swarm away from you
flashing out of the water in formation,
and boats,
sailboats with their canvas wings,
small motorboats
their back-mounted motors buzzing
like insects of legendary decibels,
and the big ones with their inboard engines,
the Cadillacs of that watery place

emerging from their houses with a self-satisfied
    rumble
to turn and breast the water,
cleaving it,
filling the air with spray,
rocking smaller boats with their waves.

Then there was the Honeymoon
a two-decker
miniature version of the larger craft
that plied the far vaster waters of Lake Michigan.
It made the rounds of the lake on weekends
tooting its train-like whistle
and announcing over a loudspeaker
"Around the lake and down the river to
    Watervliet
on the Honeymoon."
Every weekend the Honeymoon,
regular as church bells.
The boat has no doubt long since been scrapped
but it still makes the rounds of the lake in my
    memory,
its ghostly speaker calling us in its wake.
    (August 4, 2008)

Overture

The day grows light behind a scrim of haze.
A veiled sun takes the stage.
The hills across the valley still in shadow,
the river shines, serpentine,
spotlit by the sun's first rays.
Enter townsmen
going to their trades.
The music swells.
    (March 8, 2011)

County Fair

The fair has come to town
as it does this time every year,
summer fading,
foreshadowings of fall in the air,
a still hot day,
an extra-blue sky,
clouds piled high as wedding cakes.

On the fairground:
booths and rides that sprang up overnight
and will vanish just as suddenly;
cotton candy, corn dogs, pulled pork,
funnel cakes, fried dough, fried everything,
fifty-star American cuisine;
a tattoo parlor, a tarot reader,
game booths—odds favor the house—
rides with animal-shaped pods
for children to ride like joeys,
a Ferris wheel towering over all,
chairman of the rotary.

Pig races out of Tampa
just after the Republican convention there.
A man with menacing reptiles,
Kachunga and the Alligator Show.
I'm reminded of a half-blind man
I saw once in a park
displaying trained birds in a cage.
The birds sang
for coins dropped
by too few passersby.
    (September 1, 2012)

Clouds

Over the high ridge
clouds blossom
from an emptiness
of flame-blue sky,
blossom and vanish
and blossom and vanish again
in a display
of planetary
prestidigitation.
(August 1953)

The Kite

dances on air
still joined to our hand
capering to our command
its string an extension
of our nerves.
Through it we reach
cloud high
as if we rode the wind
and the whole wide sky
blew through our hair.
      (June 26, 1999)

Rowing at Evening

I like to row in evening
when dark trees
frame the still lake
and the water mirrors the sky,
to glide over the smooth surface,
stroking in slow rhythm
leaning back on the oars,
sending spirals spinning
like galaxies
into the reflected sky.
    (September 26, 1999)

Floating World

The moon,
like a Japanese lantern,
hangs from the branches of a leafless tree
on a screen of deep blue sky,
as if a print by Hokusai.
    (January 2, 2007)

Lamb-white Days

It was fine today,
this fifteenth of May,
flocks of fleecy clouds
grazing in cornflower fields
watered by yesterday's rain.
(May 15, 2010)

Rainy Evening Near the Hudson
Homage to Childe Hassam

Rain runs black on the street
down to the river
through a fringe of trees.

On the far bank
lights glitter
on the gray of evening
twined in the branches and leaves,
and lamps send yellow streamers
up the pavement.
      (September 1951)

The Bridge

It was a city like others of its time,
of low buildings
and slender steeples,
until, in its third century,
two towers of stone were raised.
Higher than any cathedral,
they could be seen
from every part of the city, and beyond,
soaring above all other works of men,
not to strive toward heaven
or flatter a capricious king
but to span a channel
between two arms of the sea.
Longer it was than any bridge before
and loftier
so that tall-masted ships
could glide beneath
as easily as gulls.
For this it was hung from cables
woven against the sky
like a web wide as a forest
in which to catch the stars.
      (November 17, 1999)

Forsaken City

Passing this small city at sunrise
I see it sleeping fitfully by its river
where once working mills lie idle
windows broken
smokestacks still.
Here as dawn breaks
I imagine hundreds
turning over in their beds
pulling the covers up,
nowhere to go today
or any day.
Yet the salmon sun
still swims up its ladder of clouds
and flights of geese slide overhead
as if this place were forest still
instead of a city turned to rust.
    (June 1, 2000)

Winter Brilliance

The geese are flying again
swiftly
after the languid slowness
of the snow,
celebrating the whitened fields
with noisy exuberance.

The geese are flying again
under blue banners
of cloud emblazoned sky.
    (December 27, 1995)

Moon Madness

Stepping out our front door
I'm suddenly awash
in the cries of geese
filling every corner
of the night sky,
silhouettes bobbing
across the lunar disk,
a crowd of shadows
driven to mad dance
by the spectacle
of a full moon
floating free
of the planet's grasp.
    (December 1998)

Birds of a Feather

Geese are military,
flying in formation,
honking in unison,
standing erect as Prussians,
their chests thrust out,
even employing a certain military gait.

Crows, on the other hand,
are anarchists.
They may fly together,
but, like bikers in bands,
each to its own beat,
emitting raucous and sardonic cries.

I think I'd rather flock with the crows.
    (January 1999)

A Chicken's Lot

Hens pattern the chicken coop,
splotches of chestnut and white,
depositing eggs
like Fabergé favors,
perfect spheroids
of perfect white,
or the soft brown
of Rhode Island Reds,
for us to gather
morning and night
still warm
from the ever-hopeful breasts.
 (July 29, 1999)

Evermore

Stepping outside I find
mere feet from my door
two large crows
in a leafless tree.
Too large for its naked branches,
motionless,
with vitreous eyes,
they look like clockwork birds,
but in their gaze I see
wary minds
appraising me.
      (January 19, 2001)

Sound Effects

I'm learning the language of birds
to conjugate their verbs
decline their nouns
as one learns a foreign tongue for the opera.

Yesterday I listened
as an oriole's aria
drilled through our windowpanes.
Later a mockingbird made it a duet.

Today despite rain I hear
songsters everywhere.
I thought the downpour would quench their
 ardor.
But no. It seems to make them
all the more boisterous.
(May 26, 2001)

Cousin Gull

Wet air has swept in from the coast
bearing gray layers of cloud
and gulls that wheel and cry
over the shopping center parking lot
(wet black like tidal flat)
searching for the fallen fry
or other delicacy,
at home with us
and our machines
as if they knew
our progenitors too
climbed from the ancestral sea.
      (November 30, 2001)

Bird Love

I love the roundness of certain wrens,
the way they hold their tails erect,
the great blue heron's elegance,
long-legged birds perched in trees,
the green heron's stubby gravity
and tunic of forest hues,
the titmouse's big eyes and jaunty crest,
the cedar waxwing, so soigné,
the flamingo's neck
for Wonderland croquet,
the blue jay's drum major uniform,
the cardinal's red cassock and ecclesiastical mien,
the downy woodpecker's piano key plumage,
goldfinch yellow glimpsed among leaves,
the oh so indigo, indigo bunting,
the junco's soothing gray,

the chickadee's pluck,
the crow's uncouthness,
robins at tug of war with worms,
woodpeckers jack-hammering trees,
cormorants hanging their wings out to dry
or paddling low in the water
like homeboys in low riding cars,
the hummingbird's powers of levitation,
the swallow's aerial ballet,
the catbird in the catbird seat,

the oriole's long, fine song,
the veery's eerie, fugal notes,
the wood thrush's haunting melody,

honking choruses of geese,
the peaceful fluting of the dove,
the eldritch hooting of the loon,
and these are just a few.
    (January 3, 2002)

Grackles

I

Grackles, with their yellow eyes
and coats of purple sheen.
seem to reflect the infernal fires.
Crows, on the other hand,
for all their Hells Angel airs,
are shabby in their shiny black suits.
Grackles, I suspect,
are Beelzebub's messengers,
crows merely his clerks.
 (May 30, 2002)

II

In the forge fire light of early morning
a grackle quarters our lawn,
spearing breakfast without breaking stride,
as if it were skewering sinners
on a field of Judgment Day.
Its black coat shines purple
like a threadbare preacher's suit,
its eye an ember yellow
like the fires of a nether place.
 (June 14, 2005)

III

New Latin Gracula...from Latin graculus, jackdaw.—
American Heritage Dictionary

Oh grackle, you seem a dyspeptic fellow
with your jaundiced eyes
and querulous cries
and coat of iridescent black
that looks like a well-worn undertaker's frock.
You seem to wear a permanent scowl.
Are you a discontented fowl?

Now why should that be?
Perhaps you're full of envy
because cousin crow is bigger.
Or could it be because men
hold you in such low regard,
go so far as to call you vermin?
But who are they,
clumsy creatures that can't even fly,
to look down on one
whose name comes straight from Latin?
    (February 15, 2009)

Crows in the Rain

I've always wondered what birds do in the rain.
Surprisingly, I've never seen.
Today I noticed a cluster of crows
hunched stoically (I imagined)
in a tree
a cold November downpour
running down their backs.
One was clucking faintly
as if in misery.
Now I don't much care for crows
but seeing them pelted with icy water
gave me a shiver of sympathy
and I wanted them to be
somehow immune
to the wet and cold.
They must be, I thought,
or they wouldn't be sitting in a tree.
But then where would they sit,
those shifty, thieving,
suffering fellow creatures?
(November 22, 2002)

Early Birds

Quarter to six a mid-May morning
the sun not risen yet
but light enough
that this bit of the world is visible
aside from where the remains of night
pool under bushes and trees.
No traffic on our street so far
nor other noticeable human stirrings.
Crows cawing down the block.
Mourning doves crooning amorously.
A woodpecker's ratta tat tat
in the woods across the way.
A finch hops out from under a shrub
and takes off with two companions.
They fly in close formation
down the empty street,
already about their business
while most of us humans
are still asleep.
      (May 17, 2004)

Geese on the Loose

Crowds of geese
over the lake
this fall fresh afternoon,
flying helter-skelter
not in neat formation
but in ragged troupes
honking raucously—
like partygoers
blowing away the old year,
tooting in the new—
joyously free,
unbound by gravity,
nowhere they need to go
nothing they need to do.
      (November 3, 2005)

Man and Dog

Long ago you decided to join our pack.
We had fire to warm you on cold winter nights
and fed you bones and scraps.
You helped us hunt,
warned of intruders
and helped us drive them away.
Later you herded our other animals.
Above all we gave each other love.
Now we walk you on a leash,
enter you in shows
and pick up your feces in plastic bags.
    (July 11, 2005)

Guinevere

Our neighbor has a setter named Guinevere
so old she puts her paws down carefully when
    she walks
but I imagine her in her prime
moving with fluidity and grace
her silky coat flowing
as she courses through fields
in search of game,
or a puppy once
before she learned to behave with dignity,
so long ago
it must seem unreal in her mind.
        (November 29, 2008)

Dogs/Cats

Dogs are outgoing
cats aloof,
dogs noisy
cats quiet,
dogs loquacious
cats laconic,
dogs transparent
cats opaque,
dogs excitable
cats cool,
dogs galumphing
cats lithe,
dogs woolly
cats silken.
    (April 22, 2016)

Room with Cats

Two bushy cats
dispose themselves
about the room,
one on the couch,
paws in air
head upside down
tracking me intently
willing me to rub its belly,
the other on a chair
under the dining table
studying, no doubt,
the secret underside of tables,
and when the chair is drawn out
rising like a lion from the grass
ravenous
for a scratch behind the ears.
    (April 17, 1999)

Cat and Geese

The air is suddenly full of geese
dozens, scores,
wave upon wave
like B29s over Tokyo,
all honking vigorously
as if fired up
by a patriotic speech.

The neighbor's cat
is racing around the house
now on his third lap
excited perhaps
by the aerial enthusiasm
or maybe unhinged
by the sight and sound
of so many fat birds
flying out of reach.
    (January 4, 2007)

Children's Story

A bee lights inside our window
this late October day.
How did it get in, I wonder.
I didn't hear it buzz by when I opened the door
see it out of the corner of my eye
feel a backwash from its wings.
But there it is on the windowpane.
What to do?
We can't live with a bee,
can we?
No, my wife wouldn't, even if I could.
(Wives are more practical.)
Were it a fly I'd swat it,
but a bee is too fine a creature for such a fate.
So I open the casement and blow
with all the force of my lungs
as if to extinguish candles on a cake
realizing, as the bee veers out
into the cold October air,
that it probably won't last the night,
that my breath is death to that bee.
Will it go knowingly, frantically wanting to live,
or is that beyond the insect mind?
Perhaps it will be numbed by the cold
and slip away anesthetized.
It's dark and getting colder now
and I wonder if the bee is already gone
or dying out there alone in the dark,
and I wish we could live with bees.

If this were a children's story
the bee would share this house with us
and we'd look upon each other
complaisantly every day
and in the spring the bee would go forth
and resume its gathering ways.
    (October 29, 2002)

Rhapsody in Butterflies

It's mostly small white butterflies again,
some with a spot or two
but still plain and unassuming.
So the season began,
though soon the warm sun hatched varied hues,
black, then sulfur, then blue,
and swallowtails,
tigers, big and boisterous yellow,
great spangled fritillaries,
like tambourines,
and monarchs swelling the season's close
with orange harmonies
and a slow, soft clapping of wings.
But now it ends as it began
returning to the simple tones
from which that grand crescendo grew.
      (September 17, 2005)

Burros

I remember the donkeys of the Andes,
those long-eared, long-lashed,
dust-covered donkeys,
shaggy and taupe,
no larger than colts
but thicker, more compact,
as if built for struggle,
seeming sweet and shy
yet capable of carrying weight
that would daunt a larger beast,
of carrying a sea chest over a mountain,
or a man, his legs spread wide,
capable of carrying heroes.
    (November 26, 2004)

Carriage Horses

lined up at Central Park South,
waiting with equine patience,
or melancholy,
heads hanging,
daydreaming perhaps
of racing across the steppes,
powering a chariot in the Hippodrome
or, splendidly caparisoned,
bearing the flower of knighthood
into the lists,
now waiting for tourists
at 59th and 6th.
    (November 20, 2009)

Apple Factory

The apple tree,
summoning its resources,
bears blossoms
and new young leaves.
Then the blossoms recede
leaving fruit buds
and the leaves deploy their solar panels
drawing from the air
the infinitesimal building blocks
of plants and anthracite and diamonds
to shape
red globes of fruit
shiny and sweet
fashioned of earth and air and rain
and the fires of the sun.
(April 24, 1999)

The Climbing Tree

The tree was tall
but made for climbing
branches close to the ground,
thick foliage
where we could perch
concealed from the world
like secret birds,
branches closely spaced
a Jacob's ladder
into the airy realm
of birds and squirrels
and the daydreams
of tree climbers.
    (June 11, 1999)

Trees

their leaves suffused with sunlight
or layered in shadow,
inert in still air
or riffled by a breeze,
boughs rising in wind
like waves on a great green sea.
What better canopy
for a world?
＿＿＿＿*(May 9, 2000)*

What the March Wind Saw

blossoms and clouds blowing white
against a blue-washed sky

aureoles of daffodils
above the winter stubble

forsythia miming sunlight
beneath the leafless trees

budded boughs cascading
from early greening willows

birds, birds, undeterred
by all the bluster and chill
    (April 3, 2002)

On the Verge

Though the trees are barren still,
nothing but naked winter wood,
and the fields are brown and bare,
it's warm today
and soon,
as soon as tomorrow perhaps,
buds will emerge amazingly,
flowers will rise out of empty ground
bushes and trees will don lacy green
and the earth will deliver
new leaves of grass.
    (March 22, 2005)

The First Flower of Spring

It was warm today, this first of April,
and I saw my first spring flower,
the only one I saw
as I walked across town,
a crocus poking bravely
out of bare ground.
(April 1, 2014)

Signs of April

It may be true
that one robin
doesn't make a spring,
but, as I took my walk today,
I saw five
pulling worms from the soil,
now thankfully thawed,

and crocuses
in nests of winter stubble
opening their mouths wide
to the sun.
      (April 4, 2008)

Mildred Munsees Spring

When I was a boy
a good many decades ago
a girl named Mildred Munsees
lived in our neighborhood,
very pale blond,
a real Rhine maiden type.
Anti-Semitic too.
I remember her up in a tree
about this time of year
hissing and spitting
arguing that it was better to be born in winter
    than spring
for she was born March 19
while I was born the 23rd.
Today, the 24th, I took a walk in the park.
It was a balmy day,
the first in weeks,
and I thought of Mildred Munsees.
    (March 24, 2004)

Spring Snow

Wet snow coats
twig, branch and bud.
Against the still black street
the waning season
limns its last words
in bold calligraphy.
    (March 31, 1997)

Rite of Spring

First it was crocuses
thrusting up
out of the bare ground
like the sound of a woodwind
piercing a silence.
Now forsythia has flared
proclaiming itself with brassy fanfare,
while from bush and tree
leaf buds emerge
pianissimo...
but building to a grand crescendo.
    (April 7, 2001)

Spring Surge

Today as I walked out
a harsh whisper of wind filled my ears
and the air was chill
but everywhere the colors of spring
dappled winter's gray palette.
Blossoms bedecked
the cherries' dark boughs,
forsythia flourished boisterously,
a shower of new leaves
enveloped trees
in fountains of pale green,
and I felt the sap within me rising.
    (April 10, 2000)

Let the Season Begin

It was as warm when I awoke this morning
as it was at dusk last night.
Blossoms and budding leaves
festooned the trees
and the streets were freshly rinsed with rain,
in readiness
for the festival
of spring.
    (April 4, 2000)

Processional

Promenaders have come again
to the path beside the lake
deserted all winter long
save for dry leaves cartwheeling in the wind
and the rare passerby
collar turned up round his chin.

Today the path flowers with fresh faces,
children running,
laughter.
In the lake fish leap,
geese glide in proud pairs,
a cormorant
emerging from a long dive
bursts into the welcoming air,
and turtles assemble
on rocks and fallen trees
celebrating the sun.
    (April 18, 2000)

Here Comes the Parade

The forsythia bloomed yesterday
yellow sprays everywhere
flying the flag of spring,
leafy regiments coming on behind,
birds piping them in.
    (April 3, 2010)

Pyrotechnics

cloudy spring day
late afternoon
satin gray sky
trees abloom
blossoms bursting
in the tingling air
like fireworks
at a county fair
    (April 21, 2001)

April Is the Cruelest Month

It looks like the last day
for the snow pile at the end of our driveway.
Once a veritable glacier
it's down to the size of a few rags
and the temperature's supposed to hit 60 today.
The whitest white at creation,
it's been dirt encrusted for weeks.
Still I'm sad to see it go,
that once proud pile of snow
reduced to a wet spot on the pavement,
crying, as its last crystal liquefies,
Oh, what a world!
What a world!
    (April 8, 2011)

Pioneer

I saw a crocus this morning
just one
in all my walk through the neighborhood,
its yellow cup thrust up
above the dirt encrusted snow,
bravely,
impudently,
and, I hope,
with foresight.
    (March 19, 2011)

Crayon Work

Colors burst from the ground
like a child's fancies,
splashes of crocus, daffodil,
hyacinth, jonquil, narcissus.
New leaves fleck trees
with diaphanous green.
Blossom clouds puff
from shrub and tree,
and forsythia challenges
a cornflower sky
with impudent graffiti.
    (April 18, 1999)

Awakenings

It's not the end of April yet
but suddenly it's summer warm.
New leaves lather trees
blossoms burst over field and yard
lawns are littered with petals and dandelions
squirrels chase one another
bees are abuzz
and my old loins stir with surprise.
     (April 15, 2002)

It's in the Air

Warm spring day.
Students from the college
out in numbers
on the green again grass
of the small park near town center,
some sitting, most lying, on the sward,
some in small groups
a few alone
but most in pairs,
and pheromones fill the air.
    (April 19, 2009)

Frabjous Day

The sky its brightest blue
the clouds their cleanest white
the air balmy
as young leaves
bedeck the trees
in their fairest green.
What a fine day to be on Earth
sailing around the sun.
    (May 28, 1999)

Firefly Time

Fireflies tonight,
first time this year.
I see them winking
where there was only darkness
   yesterday,
signals from a time
when fireflies foretold
freedom from school,
playing late in the dusk,
and the languid procession
of long summer days.
      (June 14, 2004)

Independence Day

Recurring dreamlike
through the haze of time
the tedium of those hot summer days
my back to the grassy slope
where spectators remain
bent over the ballpark
of that small town
as dusk turns to dark,
and rockets loop lazily
through the velvet air.
    (July 4, 1998)

Summer Is Here Now

as I remember it
consecrated by fireworks:
the long languorous days
tedious sometimes
but still sweet;
swimming in the lake
where skin and cool water meet
and fish dart away
from this alien invader;
water slapping on boat or dock
or weaving nets of sunlight on a boathouse wall;
the white froth of bow cleaving wave;
a sail flapping lazily as we come about;
or in a rowboat
suspended between water and sky
waiting for fish to bite;
playing into the dark hours;
and through the night
the myriad sounds of insects
and the lullaby of frogs.
    (July 7, 2001)

Summer Morning

Night having gathered the haze
woven by the heat of day
come dawn
has laid it to ground
adorning web and blade
with bright beads
while the sky,
stripped of its veils,
stuns with blue nakedness.
(May 29, 1999)

Midsummer Day

Over ninety Fahrenheit,
fans flailing in the house,
butterflies busy in the garden
extracting coneflowers' pollen cache,
a flurry of butterflies,
some a modest white
others blue
or gaudy orange,
like confetti tossed in a sudden gust.

Above the house
clouds pile high,
with the fine sheen of porcelain,
luminous in the noonday light.
The weatherman's predicting thunderstorms.
Maybe that's why the butterflies flutter so.
    (July 18, 2005)

Summer Shadows

As a breeze stirs the leaves
it seems cool
among the flickering shadows
under a lone tree or forest canopy
or in the house
where summer lingers
somnolent
in the flickering shadows.
    (May 30, 1999)

Summer Symphony

The days grow warm
then warmer,
blossoms display their petals,
clouds congeal
out of transparent sky,
thunderheads tower,
the air heaves into motion
then subsides,
drumrolls of rain
beat on fields and trees,
leaves are shaken,
puddles swell,
the sky clears,
the ground is dry again,
crops nourished
on the long summer light
grow stealthily
until one day
the corn is man-tall,
children recycle perennial games,
frogs chorus,
songsters of tree and air
do solo turns
while insects drone obbligato,
till autumn
with its melancholy airs.
    (January 1999)

Summer's End

This morning,
for the first time in months,
it was cool enough
that I felt like wearing something
next to my skin.
All the summer's haze had gathered
into a few small clouds,
hung out like newly-washed sheets,
and migrant swans came down
on the wings of the wind.
    (September 17, 1999)

Yesterday Was the Last Day of Summer

though you wouldn't have known it
from the weather.
Instead of flaunting solar splendor
the season stole away
in a cloak of gray
while today
autumn made its debut
decked out in sunshine.
    (September 22, 1999)

Autumn Road

Autumn arrived with the wind today
on a highway of clouds,
macadam grey
stretching flat bottomed
to the far horizon
through fields of flagrant blue.
(September 23, 1999)

A Time of Falling Leaves

The chill of autumn is upon us
and leaves have begun to fall,
their herb-like odor
redolent of those days
when after school
we threw ourselves
shouting and laughing
onto piles of dry leaves,
or, older, played ball
on the leaf-flecked streets
until our hands grew numb
with the cold of dusk
and we were called o
into the warm brightness
of our homes.
      (October 7, 1999)

October Morning

The hazy morning air
though honey gold
supports no bees
only dry leaves
tracing slow arabesques
to the ground.
(October 11, 1999)

It Was One of Those Fine October Days

It was one of those fine October days
free from summer's heat and haze
but not yet gripped by autumn chill.

It was one of those fine October days
when the sky's so clear
you can see the moon
through the atmosphere
at midday.

It was one of those fine October days
when the trees sport yellow and red
instead of their everyday summer green.

It was one of those fine October days
when one draws a deep breath
and is grateful
to be resident on Earth.
    (October 10, 2004)

The Beach in Autumn

I like the beach best in autumn
late October, say,
on an Indian summer day
when the vacationers have gone
and most of the shops are closed
(still displaying summer clothes),
the sand untrampled,
the sun at midday nowhere near overhead,
so you'd know it was off-season
even if you'd lost track of time.
It's being as close to alone as one can
in a place so often encumbered with crowds,
as if one had traveled back
to a time before people flocked to the shore
when coming from inland one would find
only the open sea
and sand and gulls.
    (October 23, 2009)

Green and Dying

By its coolness on the skin,
we know that fall has come
not just on the calendar
but from its cold embrace,
shriveled leaves
retreating like shades
on their way to the underworld,
green things turning brown
and shrinking into the dark ground
where they will slumber
wrapped in earth
until the season of rebirth.
(October 19, 1999)

Indian Summer

harlequin hued trees,
the fragrance of fallen leaves,
the quiet streets
of children away at school,
the sight of one's breath
in the chill of evening
or on mornings
when frost glitters
in the light
of the late-rising sun,
summer warmth suffusing
a late October day
    (October 23, 1998)

The Days Grow Shorter

It's dark now when we sit down to supper,
when I open the door on the morning paper.
Day has become parenthetical.

Leaves, dry and fractal,
slide down the curve of the season
slow-glide down Earth's arc
through air still thick with sunlight.

Soon the air will turn brittle,
harden on window panes,
and the leaves, all fallen,
will drift through the streets
like the aimless crowds of the underworld.
    (October 1, 2002)

North Wind

Yesterday north wind came
scrubbing the air blue
sending clouds scudding
across clean fields of sky
lashing leaves from trees
sweeping away summer's traces.

When I went out for the newspaper
this morning
the front door opened
on a wall of chill air.
    (October 14, 1999)

Strike up the Band

Geese have taken to the flyways,
wave after wave,
the air charged
with their ragged woodwind cries,
stirring as marching bands
striding smartly
over fall fields.
    (November 1998)

Football Weather

Leaves scuttle along the streets
like small creatures.

Fine rain falls,
barely a drizzle,
not quite cold enough for snow.

Hands on the wheel
I roll down the road
to the imagined sound of a half-time band.
    (November 8, 2010)

Autumn Riff

crews on the river,
geese overhead,
shells' glide fractioned
by oars' measured strokes,
wings beating their muffled rhythms
against a fanfare of fall foliage
and the pulsating blue
of a November sky
    (November 1998)

Autumn Sonata

Sunlight pierces the clouds
setting linden leaves aglow,
yellow as daffodils
against a dove-gray, autumn sky,
as if the seasons were juxtaposed.
And I hear music playing
on a long-ago gramophone,
the sound of strings
pressed between the years
like a blossom in the pages of a book.
            (November 11, 2000)

Those Days

I open the blinds on rain
and a chill autumn day
and am reminded all at once
of other such days,
Manhattan in the dream of youth,
Heidelberg—my time as a G.I.,
Paris on some visit,
and all those views
charged with longing and loneliness
and yellowed leaves
wetly embracing the pavement
in a parody of love.
      (November 20, 2001)

November Afternoon

   I

Patches of peach colored cloud
on a sky of rambunctious blue
adorn the end of this late November day
as the low-lying sun splashes its colors with
    abandon
on what may be
its last canvas of the season.
         (November 30, 1999)

   II

The scene's in black and white—
swaths of dark cloud,
galvanized gray sky,
crows perched in leafless trees—
save for the faint spangling
of red and yellow leaves
and a few gold streaks
squeezed from the hidden sun.
         (November 29, 2008)

Above the Valley

where old mountains slumber
grizzled and gray with leafless trees,
a counterpane
of fence-stitched meadows
glows in the parchment light
of late November
and calico clouds bedeck
a cobalt sky.
(November 29, 1998)

First Snow

Rain comes
painting a thousand mirrors
on the pavement,
a dense panorama
half formed
as in a dream.

Vehicles ply with caution
the melting streets,
the landscape in pools.

Then snow.
A man hurries by my window
his coat collar turned up round his chin.
(November 1952)

Homage to Omar Khayyam

Just before dawn
a crescent moon and Jupiter
shine in the boundless clarity
of a December sky
like a flag unfurled
over the ramparts
of morning.
    (December 3, 1999)

First Snow, December

The first month of winter
dawns on the wonder
of a whitened world.
We don't think yet
of treacherous footing,
lack of traction,
slush and grimy residue.
For now it's all joie de vivre.
Our inner child skips with delight.
    (December 1, 2012)

December Snow

Early this year,
already thicker than a featherbed,
and still falling,
the ashen sky
speckled with flakes
tumbling through the air
like millions of miniature acrobats.
    (December 9, 2009)

Season's Greetings

A card came in the mail today
on its face an old photo
of five boys running
across a snowy field in Central Park.
In the background tower the cliffs
of Central Park West
veiled in falling flakes,
as if this were a valley exempt from time,
and the boys,
their knees suspended in exuberant stride,
are wearing caps with earflaps
from that season when the world was young.
Now here in my warm kitchen
miles and years from that place
I feel its snowfield under my feet
and about my shoulders the sensation
of winter's cold embrace.
    (December 14, 2000)

Snowfall

The sun, a fiery nest
in crystal flecked haze,
is soon no more than a smudge,
embers smothered in ashen cloud.
Stillness settles
on a waiting world.
Then snow begins,
mere motes at first
speckling the sky's gray shell,
then a steady flow of flakes,
soon swarming, swirling, driving sideways,
whiting out fields, trees, houses, hills,
coiffing bush and branch,
muffling the ground
in downy layers,
wrapping us
in a cocoon of silence.
      (December 1998)

Deep Snow

Snow came during the night
padding rough fields
with sensuous curves,
burying brown stubble
in voluptuous whiteness.
Then came sunlight
sliding softly over the fresh flakes,
running its fingers
down the hills' shining flanks,
caressing the slope by the kitchen garden,
embracing the house in blue shadow.
    (February 6, 2000)

Chicago Winter

That winter the lake froze over,
ice piling up on the shore
like cards scattered
by a capricious hand.

I imagined what it would be like
walking to Michigan
sixty miles away on the far shore,
ice so wide
I would see the earth's curve,
sun-bleached sky
blending into the frozen surface
in one vast, luminous chamber,
then stars stippling an infinity of night
as if I had stepped out
into the universe.
      (September 20, 1998)

Inching up on the Equinox

It comes a minute or two closer
every day,
the fiery notches
in the ridge across the valley,
where the sun rises,
each one farther north,
the snow,
so long on the ground,
reduced to patches,
and the path by the river where I walk
soft again, ready for grass to sprout.
In a few weeks
the starkness of winter trees
will be laced with budding leaves
and the woods,
silent today,
will ring with the songs of birds.
    (March 5, 2010)

First Notes

Though winter is with us still
the birds have begun to sing
to the cues of spring,
first a cardinal, then a wren
and now this morning in early March,
as a chill dawn pinks the sky,
the wistful fluting of a mourning dove
which, after winter's longueurs,
when few but crows were heard,
now finds itself bestirred
to loose its song.
      (March 10, 2002)

Last Snow

Toward the end of the day
and nearly the end of winter
snow comes,
great webbed flakes
tumbling in profusion,
as if the skies were emptying out
the remains of the season.

Wan white soon glows on roofs
against the tinctured gray of evening.
By morning the ground
is bedded in snow
and branches are thick with whiteness.
    (March 15, 1999)

Still Delighting in Snow

I still delight in snow
seventy-some years after I first did.
Though my body now is tentative,
my spirit weary of life's contests,
I still take pleasure
in that world of whiteness
just as I did when I resided
in a frame so small
I can no longer remember how it felt.
Was I an infant?
No way of knowing,
but when I see snow fall
I sense boy-feelings
of those many decades ago,
flakes on my lashes,
the bracing scent,
the compact blizzard
as I tumbled from my sled
a scattering of cold powder
turning my eyebrows white,
as now do other causes,
my clothes encrusted
the wetness soaking through,
the warm kitchen
where I disrobed
("Get out of those wet clothes!"
my mother said)
fading
into the one where I sit now
tapping out this poem.
    (December 5, 2002)

Winter's End

This Sunday morning is less somber than the last.
A lightness ruffles the solemnity,
children's voices rising from the park
where recently the ground was shod in ice.
The clouds are taller
and sunlight peaks their summits
with a vibrant white.
A flock of pigeons flutters in the light.
The hazy air is tuned on higher strings.
    (March 19, 1952)

Everyday Things

The sky that's always with us
in light or darkness,
a radiance of moon,
the seasons,
the tree behind the house,
the birds that sing so tirelessly in its branches,
the shadow of leaves on a wall,
a spouse's touch.
Should we cherish them any the less
for being commonplace?
    (July 21, 1999)

Old Furnace

Our old furnace is being replaced,
hauled off like the belongings of a tenant
who hasn't paid his rent.
A coal burner,
it's probably been there since the house was built
nearly a century ago.
I'm old enough to remember
the coals dumped through the basement window
in a dark cloud of dust,
shoveling the shiny black lumps
into the dragon's maw,
breaking the clinkers up
face scorched by the lava glow.

Its innards were long ago replaced,
an oil burner sealed within,
but the old carapace remained
a reminder of simpler days
when we could see the fire in its gut.
      (August 22, 2006)

Smiles

Some smiles are thin,
just a crack,
some broad,
smeared across the face
like peanut butter and jelly,
some white as boxes of Chiclets,
some toothless,
at both ends of life,
some easy, sweet, warm, bright, sunny, cheerful,
welcoming, gracious, knowing, subtle,
cockeyed, loopy, twisted, wry,
prim, haughty, smug, self-satisfied,
weak, faint, tight, grim.

Next time somebody smiles at you
ask them what they mean.
    (March 14, 2007)

Pudding

There's nothing better than pudding.
Ambrosia can't hold a candle
unless
perhaps
it always was a pudding.

I even like the sound;
something embraceable,
something to curl up with
on a cold winter's night.
Better than honey
or *schatzi* or *mon petit choux*.

When I was in military school
the commandant's daughter,
a well upholstered teen,
was known among the cadets as Pudding,
Pudding Burnett.
I never learned her actual name.

Then there's the road off the Taconic,
Pudding Lane.
Every time I pass it I think
what a lovely address it would make:
Richard Greene
1 Pudding Lane
The Empyrean.
  (October 7, 2009)

Polished Stones

Beneath the leafy layers of the wood
folding green on green
the creek sings
echoing the faint, discordant tones of reverie.

Under its sinuous surface
stones glimmer
taking shape,
like words.
    (June 1996)

Poetry in the Suburbs

There's poetry in the country
with its fields and woods
and hills and waters
and welcoming sky,
and in the city
with its multitudes,
its landmarks,
its storied neighborhoods.
But in the suburbs,
among the frantic highways,
strip malls,
office parks,
overly neat subdivisions
and other conformities?

It's there.
You just have to catch it
out of the corner of your eye.
    (February 1, 1999)

The Quiet Life

Life is as quiet
as a Caribbean isle
where, always close to home,
I loll in the tropics of my leisure
in the palm groves of my mind
seldom rising from my virtual hammock
idly penning verse.
(May 1999)

The Reading

I was at a poetry reading this evening
in a room seething with smiles,
brimming with gentility.
Each member of the audience
rose to read a poem
and was rewarded with rustles of laughter
and a polite flapping of applause
for which I rarely saw good cause,
while the woman next to me
moaned her approval
at felicities I failed to perceive.
I felt as if I'd blundered
into a prayer meeting
from which I couldn't flee
without giving grave offense.
      (January 30, 2000)

Li Po

The poet Li Po,
the story goes,
trying to embrace the moon
while inebriated,
fell into a lake and drowned.
If this is so
the water would have splintered
as he struck it
into a multitude of moons.
What more fitting apotheosis
for a poet?
(April 11, 2000)

Life and Death

Of those prime themes of poetry
love and death
I'm not much interested in the latter.
Perhaps I lack eschatological fervor,
am more interested in beginnings
and prefer the ebb and flow of events
to the place where they fall off the edge.

Not that the theme lacks power.
Maybe it's that we can do nothing about it,
and I'm more interested in those destinies
we can temper.
Of death let other poets write.
I'll explore life.
    (May 29, 2000)

Confession

I'm a serial poet.
Many times I've committed poetry,
taken an image, a feeling, a thought, a phrase
and manhandled it into a poem.
I plead in mitigation
that it's a crime of passion.
Or is it temporary insanity?
    (October 30, 2003)

Painting with Words

Words are my medium.
I paint with them,
clumps of words,
tincture of words,
acrylic, tempera, fresco,
bright colored words,
words insistently monochromatic,
words full of light
or shadow,
words airy as clouds,
heavy as iron,
living words,
inanimate words,
words sumptuous and simple,
realist
expressionist
surrealist
impressionist
I lay my words on with gusto.
    (May 10, 2005)

Functional Family

I belonged to a functional family, alas,
not a good preparation for the literary life,
and was never very neurotic.
If I'd been institutionalized
they could have mistaken me for one of the staff.
So I guess memoirs are out for me
and confessional poetry.
I'll have to write about the happy life,
but what will the poetry panjandrums say?
    (March 19, 2010)

Not Much of an American

I've never cared much for baseball or beer,
sitcoms or Frank Sinatra.
I thought Gone with the Wind was dumb.
Likewise Casablanca.
Disneyland leaves me cold,
ditto Disney World
and most of the works of Walt.

I didn't like Ike,
or J. Edgar Hoover,
and Ronnie reminded me of the Wizard of Oz.
I didn't care for John Wayne either.

I don't get a kick out of waving Old Glory
and can't get hot about guys burning it.

I never got a charge out of Mustang cars
or watching NASCAR races.

I root for the underdog
not the Yankees or Dallas
or dream teams in the Olympics.

I don't believe in UFOs
or that Elvis lives
and I think school prayer should be allowed
only if it's not out loud.
As for being born again, no thanks.

Put that in your pipe, dude,
and smoke it.
    (May 20, 2000)

Progress

During the French revolution
the Marquis de Sade,
appointed as a judge,
was jailed for the crime of "moderatism"
for refusing to apply the death penalty.
We've made much progress since then
and, as always, America is on the cutting edge.
Today no law-abiding, God-fearing, right-
    thinking, pro-life American
would fall prey
to this last unspeakable perversion
of that infamous libertine.
(April 24, 2002)

Developing Eden

Eden was lost
the Good Book says,
but I'm sure that it's been found.
With man covering the earth,
by God's grace,
such fine real estate
can't be unknown ground.
I'm sure it's been improved by now.
No more lions or tigers at least
nor other dangerous beasts.
(We don't care how bright they burn
in the forests of the night.
We don't want them in our backyards.)
And no more elephants trampling.
They've been harvested for tusks.
What's more this comes with an economic plus;
Noah's ark's been downsized.
And no more dense growth to tangle our feet.
The land's been scraped and scaped
and tastefully lined with streets.
Now we can glide from one end to the other
in comfort and at ease
in our powerful SUVs.
No more meadows looking seedy.
All well-kept lawns and fairways
barred to the naked and needy.
An elegant sign now graces the gates,

> ***Eden Gardens***
> ***Residential Estates***
> *(January 3, 2001)*

After the Fall

did Eden remain the same?
I think not.
Else we could find it today.
I think it became a tangled wood,
maybe desert,
or a parking lot.
    (October 10, 2004)

A Manatee Comes to Manhattan

A manatee has been seen in the Hudson River
gawking at the tall buildings,
wondering at the absence
of mangroves and palm trees,
poking its W. C. Fields nose out of the water
as if it were about to don a top hat
and tap dance down Broadway.

This is just the beginning.
The climate's becoming warmer
the seas are rising.
Soon manatees
will crowd our summer streets
like tourists with fanny packs.
    (August 8, 2006)

Out of an Economy Endlessly Growing

This is no longer the same America, Walt,
the land you gazed upon and listened to
from the coast where it began,
a youthful land
unsure of itself, yet cocksure,
still sorting out who it was,
a slower land, horse-paced,
an aspiring land
with much to aspire to,
a land bent on nation building
with a continent to fill.

We know who we are now.
We've lived through
"the American century"
and the world emulates us,
would you believe it,
though grumbling.

The continent is now full from sea to sea
not just with homesteads, towns and cities
but with highways, some longer than the
    Mississippi
and half as wide,
satellite cities clustering around our cities of old,
housing plantations with scores of dwellings,
buildings big enough to hold a town.
With all our building
we've used up so many trees

that many of the forests you knew
have all but disappeared
and we've paved over more fields
than a thousand men could plow in a lifetime.
There are boxes in our houses and auditoriums
with pictures that move and talk.
Our space is filled with messages
that can circle the globe in an instant.
We no longer need to walk
or ride a horse or behind one
to get where we want to go,
for we have carriage-sized machines,
almost one for each of us,
that hurtle across towns
and through the countryside
at speeds that would lap
your trusty old nag
seventy times a day,
and flying machines
that leap the continent in hours!

And so we race by
the places where we used to pause
and had the time,
had to take the time,
to face those we passed
and talk with them.
Now we can travel coast to coast
talking at most
with a few toll collectors,
those who fuel our machines,

impersonal night clerks in impersonal inns
and bored youths who work in our "fast food
     restaurants".
Our eyes don't meet,
we exchange a few functional words
like putting coins in a jar,
and we're off.

All the things we aspired to,
we have them now,
as well as things you couldn't have imagined
in astonishing variety
but there's never enough.
Our appetite for things knows no bounds
and we spend more and more time
creating them
shopping for them
and enjoying them for just a short while
before moving on to the next.
And move on we do
at a pounding pace
the way you might run down a rainy street,
for fashions change now
almost as fast as the weather.

Everything is fast these days.
We work fast
we eat fast
we talk fast
we try to think and read fast
and we change our interests fast
and our trades
hurrying from one to another.

So the promise of your time
has been fulfilled
the possibilities have been realized
but where in your time
we had a few empty spaces to fill
we now have a vacuum of a strange sort.
The more we fill it
the more it grows.
    (May 5, 2000)

Angst
*Anxiety for Luxury Brands as Tiffany Reports
Slowdown*—New York Times, January 12, 2008

I wring my hands
for luxury brands.
They're not flying off the shelf
maybe not even crawling.
That's appalling.

So much love and care
invested in their shaping,
like only children,
and now they're orphans
abandoned and forsaken.

It's shocking that in this wealthy nation
our finest creations
have no takers.
We need a better safety net
for luxury market makers.
      (January 12, 2008)

Rationalizing for God

We look at the horrors of the world and say,
"How can God allow such things to happen?"
and we expend much energy
devising tortuous explanations
like Ptolemaists
struggling to keep the earth
at the center of the universe.
It's enough to make you want to hold
Ockham's razor
to a theologian's throat.
    (*April 2, 1999*)

Book and Other Worms

A medieval monk
finding a bookworm in his Bible
opined
that the worm,
having eaten God's word,
was none the wiser for it.
Are we?
       (July 27, 2007)

A Man for Some Seasons

Thomas More was amiable, intelligent
a loving father
a believer in education for girls
a man of principle.
Trouble was he martyred himself for the principle
that the bonds of marriage should never be lifted.
Likewise he participated enthusiastically in
    burning books,
and people, deemed heretical by the church.
"The devil's stinking martyr", he said of one he
    condemned,
is to go through "the short fire to the fire
    everlasting."

Was he a good man or bad?
Some of each.
    (May 7, 2009)

Angelology
White as an angel is the English child,
But I am black, as if bereaved of light.
—William Blake, "The Little Black Boy"

Now that I think of it
I don't believe I've ever seen a picture of a black
　　angel,
nor a brown nor yellow one.
I imagine there are some
but, if so, why do you so seldom, if ever, see
　　them?

I wonder too whether black angels would wear
　　white,
and whether white angels could wear black or
　　brown
For that matter, do angels have a change of
　　clothes
or do they always wear the same gown?
If so, how often do they wash it?
Do they sweat?
Do they wear underwear?

Do they eat?
Do they excrete?
(Maybe they only sip dew.)

What language do they speak among
　　themselves?
Hebrew? Latin? English?
Do they speak to each other at all?
If so, what do they talk about?
Not the weather, I hope.

Are angels evangelicals?
Do they believe in intelligent design?
Do they believe in the prosperity gospel
and that the poor are poor because they're
   feckless?
Do they read Ayn Rand?
Are they literate?
If they could vote, would they vote Republican?

Do angels in good standing, fallen ones aside,
wage war on each other?
Do they engage in crusades, jihad?
Do they belong to sects?
Do Catholic Angels make war on Protestant ones,
Sunni on Shia, Orthodox on Reform?

Do angels have genitals?
If so, why?

How many angels could stand on the head of a
   pin,
and why would they want to?
   (July 21, 2012)

Mr. Hobby Lobby
"Hobby Lobby's lawyers will argue that a commercial company can, legally speaking, be Christian — with the same rights to religious freedom that a person has."—
New York Times, August 3, 2013

Can companies be baptized?
Can they take the sacraments?
Should they have the right to marry?

Do they have souls?
Do they go to heaven or hell when they expire?

Can they be put in jail?
Can they sit on the Supreme Court?
    (August 3, 2013)

Aftermath

We were quartered in the *Heidelberg Kaserne*
a *Wermacht* billet not long before.
(Were those their beds we used
or did we bring our own?)

The town was in good condition,
spared the Baedeker raids,
thanks to the University, I suppose,
and had been sanctified since the war
by the *wirtschaftswunder,*
the economic miracle.
The natives were plump
and didn't treat us like conquerors
and we didn't play the role with them.

It was like a theme park
for young soldiers
where we could bask in the aura
of this emblematic place,
the streets of our imagination
peopled by ghostly duelists
with their trophy scars,
the actual streets
by camp followers
more hospitable even
than Disneyland hostesses;
an orderly scene
nothing like Dresden,
or after the Thirty Years War.
This storm passed over the town
preserving it as a playground
for our boys.
      (September 4, 1998)

Remembering Vientiane

Known among early European visitors
for their gentleness and insouciance,
they lingered in a backwater
of this turbulent century.

I lived in their capital
near the broad Mekong
on a dirt lane
bracketed by old wooden temples,
unpainted and weather-stained,
with their muffled bells
and slow traffic of orange-robed monks.

Only roosters
disturbed the peace
until tanks came
clogging the narrow streets,
grinding them under ridged treads,
spewing manic metal
onto roofs and shutters,
like the rhetoric
of clashing ideologies.

And bodies erupted
from the river's smooth surface.
(January 1999)

The Veterans

Of all the young men
who went to war
over half a century ago
still believing
in everlasting love
and life too long to think about,
confident they would return,
though only some did,
and confident they would get ahead,
though only some did,
many have fallen
from the ranks.

Of those who remain,
the hard muscles
that propelled them
across the fields of death,
and life,
have shrunk,
and their muscular ambitions
have withered.
Now they look back
and remember those days
when they went to war
fit and trim
and felt they could outrun mortality.
    (May 28, 1999)

All the Brave Men

The soldier's glory
is the widow's, mother's, grief.
The shot that hits its mark
stops the heart
of a husband, father, brother, son.
The bomb that interdicts supplies
takes life from those who never wanted war.
The cannon is callous
in its choice of targets
disinterested as a beast of prey
in its choice of a meal.
(August 11, 1999)

Where Have All the Young Men Gone?

Each someone's beloved
snuffed out
in the paddies of Nam
in the hills of Korea
on the beaches of Normandy,
swallowed by the greedy god
but leaving behind
those who remember
one who was
and always will be
young
embalmed in a long-ago moment
but living still
in the hearts of those
who loved him.
      (January 5, 2000)

The Grenade

A handy thing the grenade.
An ergonomic weapon.
Fits nicely in a man's hand.
Neither too heavy nor too light.
Good for throwing.

Named after the pomegranate,
because of its shape,
but might as well be because of the seeds it
    contains,
sowing death or at least dismemberment.

It's an economical weapon too
disposing efficiently
of whole groups of enemy
rather than trying to make them dead one by
    one.
It's a disassembly line.

Grenades don't help us win, however,
for the enemy has them too.
The same might be said for most weapons.
They help us only as long as they're new,
which is seldom for long.
But we have to retain them even then
to meet the competition
lest we suffer insolvency
in the marketplace of death.
    (May 13, 2000)

The Weapons Economy

Measured in weapons
human progress has been great.
Our weapons are more ingenious
effective
efficient
reliable
precise
deadly
user friendly
than ever before.

Our anti-personnel weapons
spew projectiles
as if they were ladling out beans.
Our bombs can fly through a door or window
without touching the frame.
They can pinpoint a man on a toilet seat
or the toilet seat under the man.
In the dark they home in on heat
like mosquitoes.
We can blow up cities in a flash
turning populations into toasted marshmallows.

Our gross national destructiveness has soared.
    (May 14, 2000)

A Boy's War

I was seven
when it began,
Anschluss, then Munich—
Kristallnacht slipped by
wholly unnoticed by me—
and within a year
blitzkrieg was loosed on Europe.

Then Dunkirk and the fall of France.
I heard the news on the radio,
but it didn't seem so momentous.
It was part of life as I knew it,
along with boyhood fantasies
like the warplanes I drew
and learned to recognize
daydreaming of playing the hero one day
by spotting an enemy.

If it hadn't been for my parents' hushed tones
even Pearl Harbor might have seemed
like some extravagant sports event,
for in my boyish mind
death was unreal,
and war a game.
    (September 9, 2000)

The Charms of War

It was a good war,
World War I,
for us Americans
who were in it only briefly
and didn't lose so many young men.
It had its compensations,
its mademoiselles,
its Hemingway,
old Europe
with its worldly charms,
and our heroically coming to its rescue.
Then tickertape parades
down lower Broadway,
and the best of times
in left bank cafés.
Would we have been there
if not for the war?

Then World War II
less romantic, true,
but righteous,
a war against evil,
the best of wars.
And even less virtuous wars,
food for nostalgia even there,
for we love war
and will, I suppose,
as long as men grow from boys.
    (May 11, 2001)

In Memory of

Another World War II pilot gone.
Obit on a back page of The Times
"Pilot who downed Yamamoto dies at 84."
A photo of three lean young men in khakis
looking as if they never could be 80
posed in front of a fighter plane
Pacific palms in the background.
He began high school about the time I was born
and I began it the year he downed the infamous
    admiral.
My cousin Bob was a fighter pilot in that war,
so much a part of my adolescent imagination,
and it's almost as if the young man in the photo,
now, unbelievably, deceased,
were my kin.

Obit the same day for Percy Goring, 106,
last British survivor of Gallipoli.
When I was a boy it was the last veteran of the
    Civil War
and, when a young man, the Spanish American.
For earlier generations it was the Revolutionary
the Hundred Years, the Punic, the Persian,
always one within reach of living memory,
and always some last veteran
to nurture
nostalgia for old wars.
    (August 1, 2001)

I Was a Soldier Once

I was a soldier once, and young,
though I never fought in a war,
no buddy of mine died in one
and indeed I don't remember
that any Americans fought in those years
or even if there was a war at the time.
I was a peacetime soldier,
drafted,
with no dreams of glory,
though I came to dream of waging war
on the military mind.
Oh, there were intelligent ones
but they took care to hide their intelligence.
It was OK to be smart,
but thoughtful, no,
nor inclined to see things in shades of grey.
Decisive was the ticket—
though it didn't matter where that decisiveness
    led—
respectful of tradition and authority
and the primate hierarchies of rank.
So it was a time of disgruntled draftees
overeducated and disdainful
hating every minute of their military lives,
and I was one.
But I survived.
    (November 28, 2003)

The Things They Carry

I hear casually booming voices in the street
and, looking out the window, see
two boys in their early teens.
From the sound they might be men,
and I think of such almost-men
some will grow up to be soldiers,
carry their childhood fantasies
into the world,
like flags,
and I think,
in another part of that world
these men-children would bear arms,
kill and be killed
before becoming men.
What could be more manly?
    (August 25, 2004)

Memorial

Reading the name
of a young man who died in war
saddens us.
Yet more the names of thousands
engraved in granite, or marble,
their parents' hopes and dreams
interred in stone.
All that remains are a few keepsakes,
and memories
of newborns, toddlers, vulnerable boys,
youths becoming men,
those now sad memories,
and names carved in cold stone.

Who wanted those wars?
Their leaders of course,
but all too often those same young men,
and all too often
those who mourn for them.
    (September 9, 2004)

Memorial Day
Hopewell, New Jersey, May 2005

It was enough to make us weep,
half a dozen veterans of the last great war
looking like fading away,
followed by the high school band,
booming bravely into adulthood.
Next a squad in Civil War uniform,
harking back to the source of the holiday,
a fratricide that seems today
to have occurred in another country,
not just another century.
A retired Humvee
with a small girl in back
wearing a grunt-style cap
and waving mechanically;
vintage cars,
big ones from a century ago
with wooden spokes
and other vestiges of their carriage genes,
still boxy ones from the 20s,
the streamlined 30s,
the fishtailed 50s,
a couple of Mustangs, an early Corvette;
then the fire engines, big and bigger,
like armor-plated rhinos,
our town's brigade riding old fashioned red,
others yellow,
sage green from a well-heeled town nearby;
delegations of Boy Scouts, Cub Scouts, Brownies,
one scout troop with a five-piece band

trying like twenty-five;
a motorcycle club,
plenty of paunch and gray hair,
and, though some ponytails,
suburban angels rather than Hells.
Finally, a platoon of kids
all safely helmeted,
one tireless on a pogo stick
others on scooters and bikes
and even a few on tricycles,
training for future wars.
    (May 29, 2005)

Boots on the Ground

Put boots on the ground, they said,
as if they were dragons' teeth
which, sown, sprout spectral armies
that fade away once battle is done,
leaving no blood behind.

They said nothing about
the men and boys
who would no longer have feet
to wear those boots,
or would wear them to their graves.
    (October 22, 2005)

December 7, 1941

For the young the war was far away,
something happening in Europe,
something vague.
School was more real,
Freddie Appleton's house,
our meadow,
the orchard,
the pond.

Then that day
it invaded our home,
the voices on the radio
somber, hushed,
solemn, stentorian, outraged.
My father was on the phone
talking in urgent tones.
He was activated,
reporting for duty the next day,
and we would follow him,
exiled from Eden
through no sin of our own.
    (November 20, 2005)

September 1, 1939

Where was I?
At home in our tranquil suburb?
In school, or was it too soon?
Playing with friends?
Reading in my room?
Still at the lake perhaps
or on a train
coming home.
I don't know what time of day it was,
don't think I even heard the news.
My parents surely knew
but they must have said
best not tell the children.
Nor did I know of Kristallnacht
Anschluss
the Sudetenland
Munich.

It was probably summery still,
the leaves unchanged,
a calm September day.
      (March 10, 2007)

The Unnamed Dead

"Car Bomb Kills 7 in Baghdad"
reads the headline in *The Times*.
Just a number.
We see them every few days,
these numbers,
sometimes small enough to count on your
    fingers,
sometimes a good deal larger.
Nothing but numbers,
no names,
no history.
Our military casualties
are listed daily
under the heading "Names of the Dead"
with rank, unit, hometown.
But those civilians,
just not news,
hardly even people.
    (May 13, 2010)

Your Grandfather's War

Your grandfather fought in "the great war".
He was in a famous battle in France
wounded with shrapnel and mustard gassed,
may have shot at the enemy and been shot at—
I never asked—
may even have fought hand-to-hand
where you can see the grime on your enemy's
   face
and the fear in his eyes
over the frantic thrust and parry of your bayonet
and his
and feel the frenzy of your own fear.

Now that war is history
so remote you can read of it
innocent of the feelings
of those who faced each other
in an effort to kill
and survive.
   (December 29, 2010)

Numbers Don't Speak

Sectarian Attack Kills 15 in Nigeria
the headline said.
Lots of headlines.
Five or fifteen dead,
fifty, five hundred,
a hundred thousand.
Sixty thousand the government says.
One hundred and fifty thousand
say human rights activists.

Numbers, just numbers.
It's hard to care.
Numbers don't breathe,
or stop breathing.
Numbers don't have mothers or fathers
brothers, sisters, children, husbands, wives.
Numbers don't speak
or stop speaking.
Numbers don't tell their stories.
No stories are told of them.
They're just numbers
It's hard to care.
      (January 8, 2012)

To Those without Whom We Couldn't Win

The patriots, the hawks,
the pundits, the editorial writers,
the legislators, the advisors,
all those brave men who spur us on
and hold our coats and cheer.
Without them how could we ever win a war?
    (April 12, 2012)

Beauty and Truth

Though the beautiful can be true.
and the true beautiful,
truth is often ugly
and beauty often blinds us to the truth.
Life isn't as simple
as we'd like it to be.
　　　(March 5, 2000)

Of Frogs and Toads

Kiss a frog, the tale goes,
and you may find a prince.
Kiss a toad
and what do you get?
A disgusting taste in your mouth.
Uncooked frogs, of course,
aren't very appetizing either,
but we're willing to swallow our distaste
to elevate our social status.
    (July 25, 2005)

The Competitive Society

Why does everything have to be a competition?
Getting into kindergarten for a start.
Then no longer good enough
to just enjoy playing ball.
Have to be in Little League.
Not sufficient to please teacher or parent
with orthographic prowess.
Must compete in spelling bees.
And if a pretty child
you may be tarted up
and entered in a beauty contest.

Bird watchers vie
to amass the longest lifetime lists.
Yoga practitioners strain
to be the best contortionists.

Even poetry's no longer just an individual art.
You can participate in slams
and be awarded points,
or not.
And serious poetry
has become a competition
to be the most arcane.
It's a zero-sum game.

Slackers, even, now compete
to see who can be the slackest.
    (September 11, 2006)

Yom HaShoah

"Yidn, schraybt!"
"Jews, write!"
the historian
Simon Dubnow
cried out
as he was led away to die,
Riga
December 8, 1941.
And write we did,
Anne Frank
Primo Levi
Elie Wiesel,
too many to remember here.
Then came the others
to write that thousands lied,
David Irving
Mahmoud Ahmadinejad
David Duke.
Why?
      (January 7, 2007)

Earthquake, Port-au-Prince, 2010

If we could hear all the cries from Haiti
we'd clap our hands over our ears
our faces twisted in pain.
If we could hear all the cries
from around this world
on almost any day
we'd be pressed to the ground
as if by a raging hurricane,
but we've learned not to listen,
or maybe never learned to hear.
    (January 15, 2010)

Nothing New

Tonight a year ends.
Some will see it out tooting and hollering.
Not us.
My wife's already in bed
and I'll join her there soon.
Were it not for this poem
I'd be in my armchair reading,
my eyelids succumbing to gravity,
and my head may yet be on its pillow
before the clamorous hour.

Suppose there were no years.
Would anything be different?
We think important things have ended and
    begun
when it's only a matter of digits on a calendar,
perhaps some resolutions,
largely to be unfulfilled,
or the earth beginning
another of its innumerable circuits around the
    sun.

The world doesn't stop at midnight
like a train changing engineers.
There's no bump in the road of time.
The scene hasn't changed.
The characters remain the same.
The play goes on as before.
Dramatic climax is no more likely
at this moment than any other.

There isn't even an intermission.
A foot raised at the end of one year
comes down the next
with no pause in between.

But, as the planet circles its star,
at a certain point in its orbit
where it's arbitrarily said to have started,
humans bellow and hug their fellows,
as if this carousel hadn't gone around
a few billion times before.
    (December 31, 2011)

Mankind and Moonshine

Alcohol no doubt was discovered by accident
like penicillin and many another important
    innovation.
Maybe it was discovered more than once,
reinvented like the wheel.
Somebody left some beverage lying about,
it fermented
and another, thirsty, came along and chugged it
    down.
Or maybe it was fruit fallen to ground,
a bunch of grapes, an apple.
Maybe original sin wasn't a bite at all
but a slurp of fermented windfall
and man thought being stoned a source of
    insight,
as we still do.
    (October 24, 2012)

The Afterlife of Gods

What happens to gods
when people stop believing in them?
Do they expire,
or live out their eternities
in some special limbo
for the late divine?

Though we don't recognize them by name,
some may live on in the hearts of men,
confined spaces, to be sure,
but widespread.
Mammon, of course.
Mars, Venus, and Bacchus too.

But what of Baal, Ra, Zeus, Thor,
Quetzalcoatl,
and all the others?
Are their immortal remains
shrunken and shriveled
like sun-dried fruit,
or do they survive in fine form
playing endless rounds of golf
in some other-worldly
retirement community?
    (January 1999)

Faking It

Trying to look all knowing
when you haven't got a clue,
Trying to look full of confidence
when you don't know what to do,
Trying to look like you meant to do
what was really a stupid mistake,
Trying to look wise and witty
when you don't know what to say,
Trying to look like you're singing along
when you're not very sure of the words,
Trying to look like you know the dance
when you haven't learned the steps,
Looking around for a bump in the floor
when you've stumbled over your feet,
Trying to look like you got the joke
when you don't know what's so funny.

Trying to look on top of the world
when you're really down in the dumps,
Trying to look cool
when you're seriously insecure,
Trying to look like a racing car driver
when you have no power to spare,
Trying to look like a VIP
when you're just a face in the crowd,
Trying to look like Schwarzenegger
when you're more like a 90-pound weakling.

Trying to look like a blond
when at root you're a brunette,
Trying to look 21

when you're barely 17,
Trying to look 35
when you're pushing 53,
Trying to look like you've got a full house
when all you have is a pair,
Trying to look like you have two pairs
when you've got a royal flush,
Trying to look all innocence
when you're lying through your teeth.

Trying to look like you're sober
when you've had a few too many,
Trying to look wide awake
when you're nearly falling asleep,
Trying to look like you're enjoying yourself
when you'd really rather be home,
Trying to look like you're all ears
when you haven't heard a word,
Trying to look deeply concerned
when in fact you couldn't care less,
Trying to look like you couldn't care less
when you're actually knocked for a loop,
Trying to look like you're not trying at all
when you're jumping through all the hoops.
    (March 1999)

The Hospital Poem

My muse sidled up to me
as I lay in my hospital bed
and tapped me on the arm.
Write a poem about being in the hospital, she
 said.
It's hard to write lying on your back, I said.
Besides, what's to write about?
You can write a poem about anything, she said.
Hospitals are the antithesis of poetry, I said,
you're wheeled about
poked and prodded
cut open and sewn up
stuffed full of things
like a culinary concoction,
and you're always on your back
looking at the ceiling
or others' heads and shoulders
as if you inhabited an upside-down universe
while everyone around you
is privileged to live upright,
and what with the noise
you couldn't sleep
even if they didn't wake you
five times in the night,
and the food tastes like it's been through the
 laundry.
No wonder the wards are filled with moaning.
And all those bodies being jockeyed around on
 gurneys,
like some kind of carcass race,

crowds of visitors coming and going—
you'd think they'd come to see a show—
attendants bustling
as if their exertions
kept the world turning,
and the strange words that fill the air
osises and itises and otomies and ectomies
like the buzzing of insects.
How is one to make any sense of it?
There you go, she said.
    (April 8, 2000)

Existentially Speaking

If you want to elevate your discourse
just add "existential".
That dignifies the commonplace with profundity.
Dyspepsia, for example, is merely heartburn,
but existential dyspepsia
is a much more significant condition,
an inability to stomach the world.
It's like the difference between sorrow
and worldsorrow (*Weltschmerz*, as they say).
Sorrow is sadness about something
but *Weltschmerz* is all-embracing.
Weltwhatever, by the way,
is almost as good as existential,
or at least it used to be.

Then there's existential halitosis,
not bad breath
but a moral condition.
This is not an attribute of great villains
destined for eternal notoriety,
but of those merely of foul odor,
Rush Limbaugh, for instance.

Existential flatulence,
for a final example,
is not a mere fart
but a matter of what you have to say
or how you say it.
Many a poetry critic is afflicted with this
    condition,
and those who make much use
of the word existential.
    (September 23, 2000)

Hello, Is Polly There Please?

The phone rings a few minutes after nine.
A young woman's voice,
a lovely voice,
could be that of a radio announcer,
a TV anchor,
contralto
forceful
self-confident
perfectly modulated
as if she'd been rehearsing this moment for
    weeks,
training for it for a lifetime,
practicing to get the voice just right
for this call
to a wrong number.
    (February 16, 2011)

Timepieces

the hourglass,
its thread of sand
extruding the perfect cone
voluptuous as a dune
in the far Sahara

the sundial
harnessed to our fierce star
with soft shadows,
rotating solemnly
on the planetary axis

the clock,
its winking wheels
winding down the segments
of our days

steadfast, quiet,
sweet instruments of time
measuring out our moments
with lyrical precision
    (October 1998)

The Sun and the Moon

The sun
either burns with righteous anger
or turns its face from us
as if unable to bear
our nocturnal debauchery.
The moon, on the other hand,
regards our antics with equanimity,
a smile lighting
its dissipated pallor.
The moon is sardonic,
the sun, well, intense,
but the sun,
as they say of virtue,
triumphs,
effacing its unwelcome interlocutor
in a cleansing auto-da-fé.
By nightfall, however,
the moon is back,
like that phoenix
called human nature.
      (December 13, 1998)

Tall Ships

The words evoke
banks of sails
heavy with air,
majestic as chalk cliffs
or the baroque brilliance
of summer clouds,
great blades
of weathered wood
peeling back
a white skin of water,
baring its black core,
the hoarse whisper
of a hull
cleaving through
complaisant waves,
or its frantic creak and rumble
under the frenzied drum-roll
of a stormy sea,
crewmen climbing
the towering trees
of mast and rigging
in sunny calm
or apocalyptic tumult,
above the sea's capricious grace.
(November 1998)

Islands of the Mind

We dwell on islands
gathering our world about us
striving to order it to our whims.
We think of ourselves as one of a kind
(despite the other footprints in the sand)
unique in our joys and sorrows,
seeing justice only in our cause,
laying the template of our meanings
on others' words,
alone in knowing what is good and true
and beautiful.
The poet was wrong when he said
no man is an island.
We are all islands,
in our minds.
    (March 1999)

Wild Things

Give thanks for wild things,
here in our suburban fastness,
for squirrels and deer and rabbits
woodchucks and raccoons,
for woods and forests
wind and fire
and for our untamed urges.
    (July 19, 1999)

Of Roosters and Motorcars

I've dwelt in cities
where roosters still crow
or bells still toll
to welcome the dawn
or call the faithful
to their devotions,
waking us with their cries and clangor.
I've dwelt in cities
where muezzins' chants
announce the early prayer
and on the Sabbath
rival bells in their clamor.
And I've dwelt in cities
where the only sound
is that of motorcars
lulling us with their hum,
but I prefer the waking to the lull.
    (September 7, 1999)

The Bag

A plastic bag
pirouettes on the highway,
performs protracted jetés
in the wind of passing cars,
unperturbed
by the massive machines
hurtling by,
as if no place could be more natural
for a ballet.
  (October 26, 1999)

The Bear

I found a worn teddy bear in our attic,
one half-remembered
as if only a dream.
When I squeezed it
it played a lullaby,
a tune I remembered
without knowing its source,
and with that tune came back
a time before memory
a time I knew only from photographs:
of my mother
younger than I could recall
smiling with pleasure at me,
of myself still bald and stubby legged,
or lofted gleefully on a teeter-totter
or a bit later
posed and pensive
with a halo of light brown curls.

For years that bear
lay in its box
waiting for me to pick it up,
that bear I can no longer find.
    (November 29, 1999)

The Inner Child

I know I'm a different person than I was
in my youth
but sometimes it doesn't feel that way.
It's as if all my mistakes had happened yesterday
and could happen again tomorrow,
as if I were like a tree
growing by adding layers
with all previous versions nested inside.
Am I unusual in this?
I doubt it.
We think our faults unique
when actually they're common as grass.
There's been much talk in recent years
of the inner child
as if this were a part of us
that's still spontaneous and pure,
when in fact it is, like the original,
full of insecurities and needs
and clamoring for gratification.
    (February 16, 2000)

Words

What are words?
Mere marks on a surface,
or maybe shallow grooves
but often nothing more
than a slight disturbance of the air
less palpable than a breeze.
Yet they propel us through our world
as furiously as any hurricane.
    (*October 9, 2001*)

Intimate Strangers

How little we know our fathers and sons
who conceal their innermost thoughts
as men and boys are wont to do,
those with whom we dwell a near score years,
whose DNA coils in our cells
and ours in theirs,
root and branch of the same tree.
How little we know of their desires,
    disappointments,
losses, loves,
failures, fantasies, fears
of how they see us
and whether we see them as they are.
And how little they know of us.
    (September 26, 2002)

Wind

The air that has lolled for days
on earth's green cushion
bestirred itself today
stretched its long limbs
heaved an immense sigh
and launched itself over the town
jostling branch and blossom
spanning leagues
with each beat of its wings.
    (July 12, 2003)

I Hear Its Whistle

I hear its whistle probe the night
as if it were probing time.
I hear its wheels rumble
down the livelong line.

Time was when trains were everywhere,
their whistle and rumble and clack.
Now it's the sound of cars and trucks,
their hiss and buzz and whine.

When I hear a whistle in the night
I search in my dreams for that lost time.
     (February 17, 2004)

Thinking of Teachers

Miss Kenyon was my third-grade teacher.
I've wondered recently what became of her.
I don't remember what she looked like
or even her first name,
but I wonder if she married and had children of
　her own.
If she did, they'd be middle aged now, or older,
and she most likely deceased,
though in my mind she's perpetually young.
She wasn't married then, I know,
since she was Miss Kenyon, not Mrs.
In those days you could tell.
At the time I didn't think of adults as sexual,
though I already knew about sex.
They were just teachers and parents
aunts and uncles,
shopkeepers and the like.
I never thought of them as making love,
but I wonder now.
　　　(May 26, 2004)

Where Are You Now, Shirley Temple?

with your upbeat songs
and sunny curls
and dimples that could wish the world's cares
　　away?

Not in some nursing home, I hope,
halo dimmed with blue rinse,
watching movies in your head
and smiling at cameras no longer there.

The world is coming undone,
warming at an ominous pace,
fish fast disappearing from the seas,
terrorism a plague.
Where are you Shirley Temple,
now when we need you most?
　　　(July 15, 2005)

The Theater Is Closed

I mourn the Yiddish theater,
already in decline
before I,
California born,
was even aware it existed.
I learned of it
when we moved to New York
and I went with my mother
to the Lower East Side
for pastrami, corned beef, lox
and other deli delights.
I'd see the billboard signs for plays,
with Jacob Adler, Boris Tomashevsky, Molly
   Picon,
alien to me as Chinese opera,
I who know little Yiddish,
a smattering of words and phrases
pungent but quaint.

I mourn that stewpot of emotions
simmering off stage as on,
those old-world theater people,
with their soap opera lives,
aspiring to higher art,
the audiences with their old-country minds
seeing their unmoored lives reflected
in the shimmering pool of stage,
all those for whom that theater
was real as life.
    (January 2, 2007)

Old Barn

There's an old barn
not far from our house
that's nearing the end of its days.
Its boards are scoured and scored
its roof sags
and there are yawning holes in its sides.

When it was raised
the neat lines of its frame
stood firm against the sky
and it was clad in clean young boards and paint.

Once workmen, with their laughter, came storing
   hay
children played in its loft
and young people experimented there with love.

Once cows and horses sheltered between its
   walls
and gave birth there to their young
mice scurried along its beams
swallows and owls nested under its eaves
and cats came to prowl and prey.

Now the barn is an empty husk
and the fields from which it gathered its hay
have reverted to scraggly woods and scrub.
   (January 9, 2007)

The Voices of Stones

Who can look on Ayers Rock
without hearing songlines,
Stone Mountain
without Dixie or the Battle Hymn
ringing in one's inner ear,
Angkor or Machu Picchu
without phantom voices,
boulders without mountains' deep bass,
pebbles without the murmur of streams?
Who says that stones are mute?
They whisper, babble, boom, chant, sing.
    (February 25, 2008)

Sunday on the Bike Path

A runner passes
bobbing like the needle
on a slow-moving sewing machine,
flickering in the sunlight
that falls through the trees,
as if dematerializing,
diminishing
till he's not much larger
than an exclamation point.

I stop to talk to a dog.
Her name is Sadie
her owner says.
Friendly name for a dog, I say.
I stop for a fuzzy cat.
It looks severe
but, uncatlike,
comes right up to me.
Charlotte its name tag says.
Clearly a feline of lineage.

Bicyclists pass,
some properly uniformed
in Star Trek helmets and spandex,
some violating the dress code shamelessly,
families with kids on small bikes,
littler ones in child seats and trailers,
like passengers in limousines,
guys with babes
deeply décoletéd,
some with mates more sedate.

I walk, don't ride.
My wife took my bike away
for my eightieth birthday.
You're too old to bike, she said,
I don't want to have to take care of you
if you fall and break something.
Bye bye bike
after all these years
my biking days finis.
Got no ticket to ride,
but I don't care.
The bike path's still there
and I can ambulate,
as my stepfather,
born in 1895,
was fond of saying,
on shanks' mare.
   (September 18, 2011)

TRANSLATIONS

Ave Atque Vale—Catullus (c84-c54 BCE)

Through many lands and over many seas
I come, brother, to this sad ceremony,

to confer on thee this final service to the dead,
and address in vain your mute ashes.

Since fate has taken thee from me,
Oh, brother, torn away too soon,

I give thee these last offerings,
blessed by the tradition of our fathers.

Accept them, though sodden with fraternal tears,
and, for eternity, brother, hail and farewell.

VIII—Catullus (c84-c54 BCE)

Wretched Catullus, may you cease playing the
 fool,
and recognize that what once was is no more.
Once the sun shone for you
when you with your mistress rendezvoused.
Such love you'll never see again.
You made merry as you would
and she too not unwillingly.
Truly the sun shone for you.
Now that she spurns you,
you (though besotted still) should spurn her too.
Don't run after her, nor let misery get the better
 of you.
Be firm.

Farewell, mistress. Catullus is determined.
He won't pine for you.
He won't come knocking at your door.
You will suffer when no one wants you anymore.
Woe to you wicked girl!
What life is left for you?
Who will visit you?
Who will exclaim over your looks?
Who will pamper you with love?
With whom will you be paired?
On whom will you lavish your kisses?

Whose lips will you nibble now?
But you, Catullus, be firm.

An Old and Distinguished Gentleman—Antonio Machado (1875-1939)

I've seen you, in the ashen park
the poets love
for weeping, like a noble shadow
stray, enveloped in your long frock coat.
The courteous manner,
formed so many years ago
one holy day in the antechamber
—how well your poor ceremonious
bones do their duty!—
Today, tepid afternoon in which the humid wind
tears loose the withered leaves,
I've seen you inhaling distracted,
with the breath the earth exhales,
from the green eucalyptus
the freshness of the perfumed leaves.
I've seen you lift your dry hand
to the pearl that shines on your cravat.

November 1913—Antonio Machado (1875-1939)

One more year,
the sower again casting seed
over the earth's furrows.
Two slow teams of oxen plow
while overhead pass ashen clouds
casting shadows on the countryside,
the freshly plowed fields
the grey olive groves. At the valley bottom
a turbid river rises.
Cazorla has snow.
and Mágina, a storm,
Aznaitín its cap. Toward Granada,
mountains with sun, mountains of sun and stone.

Autumn Day—Rainer Marie Rilke (1875-1926)

Lord. It is time. The summer was so bountiful.
Lay thy shadows on the sundials
and let the winds loose on the meadows.

Bid the last fruits be full;
give them yet two southerly days,
press them to fulfillment and drive
the last sweetness into the heavy wine.

Who now no house has, will build himself one no
 more.
Who now is alone, will long remain so,
will wake, read, write long letters
and restlessly wander the boulevards
back and forth, as the leaves are driven.

Black Cat—Rainer Marie Rilke (1875-1926)

A ghost is like a place where
your sight stumbles with a thump,
but in the cat's dark fur
your most steadfast stare will dissipate,

as a madman in full frenzy
thrashing in his dark cell
suddenly stops before the padded wall
and is pacified.

She seems to hide on herself
every look she encounters
in order, sullen and menacing,
to watch over and sleep with it.
But suddenly, she turns her face to yours,
as if awakened:
and you encounter,
unexpected, your glance,
imprisoned in the amber of her eyes
like an ancient, extinct fly.

www.ingramcontent.com/pod-product-compliance
Lightning Source LLC
Chambersburg PA
CBHW072041160426
43197CB00014B/2575